The Roadmap to a Profitable $30 Million Real Estate Business

How to Build Wealth and Live a Balanced Life

By
Reeta Casey and Rick Ruby

Published by The CORE Training, Inc.

Edited by Kelly Zientek

Additional acknowledgments of the efforts from:
Marvin King, Tenille Norris, and Kelli Mattison

Visit our website at www.thecoretraining.com

CONTENTS

FOREWORD

How do you say "thank you" to the people who have changed your life? The limited space afforded to me in this foreword is insufficient to fully express my gratitude for what Rick Ruby, Reeta Casey, Todd Scrima, and The CORE Training have done for my family and me.

If you ask most successful athletes who was the most impactful person in their life, they will often talk about their coaches. When you ask about their best coaches, they refer to the toughest and most demanding.

THE CORE focuses on three things: systems, structure, and accountability. Systems are the processes and checklists that are essential to running a business and delivering great customer service. Structure is how the business grows profitably and operates with balance. Accountability is the boss or the coach. We all need that boss or coach to hold us accountable. It is accountability that turns dreams into goals, goals into action, and action into results. The result of applied systems, structure, and accountability is a profitable business with a balanced life. That combination gives us an opportunity to "pay it forward."

The best coaches demand the best results, and the best coaches expect and get more out of their players than anyone else. The best coaches lead by example, show love, earn respect, and challenge you to be the best you can possibly be, which is usually way beyond your personal expectations.

The best coaches are impactful and influential, and they get the greatest results. The best coaches hang with you through the tough times and celebrate with you in the good times. The best coaches let the light shine on you.

My coaches, Rick, Reeta, and Todd, have done all that and more for me. The CORE has helped me grow my business exponentially. More than that, I have been challenged to be a better husband, father, friend, student, steward, giver, saver, manager, leader, and servant.

We all are born with the opportunity to change someone's life for the better. Rick, Reeta, and Todd are making the most of that opportunity. I will always be grateful for their leadership and friendship and for recognizing the potential in me way beyond my wildest dreams.

Thank you all. You have changed my life!

Dayton Schrader
RE/MAX Associates, San Antonio, Texas
Broker Associate CCIM, CRS, CRB, CLHMS, CDPE, ABRM

Dayton Schrader has been a real estate professional with RE/MAX in San Antonio since 1982. Dayton met Rick and Reeta in 2000 and has been a student and coach for The CORE Training since 2001. Since then, Dayton has built a team to help him grow his business from $15,000,000 in sales to over $100,000,000 in annual sales.

REETA CASEY: INTRODUCTION

Do you love being in real estate sales, but hate the long hours? Do you find yourself burning out from constant stress and 24/7 chaos? On top of all of this, are you tired of working hard and making sacrifices, but not making the money you need to support your family?

If your answer to any of these questions is "yes," then this book is for you. I wrote this book specifically to help you restructure your business. I will teach you The CORE Training's systems for building a profitable real estate business while maintaining life balance and building personal wealth. There is no reason you can't enjoy every day of your career and still have time for yourself, your family, and your friends. We want to teach you how to build financial freedom while working in the real estate business.

The information in this book is derived from my 27 years of experience in the industry, but more importantly, the results I achieved in the last 15 years under the coaching of my CORE partner, Rick Ruby. He taught me how to think like a businessperson versus a salesperson, which transformed my business and my life.

These CORE systems and business tactics work in any sales business. The sooner you "surrender" and realize that they can be applied in real estate, the sooner you are on your way to changing your business and life. As you read this book, be sure not to over think or complicate the methods as described. What I love about

Rick is he keeps everything simple and straightforward. We have taught these principles for 15 years, and our students have proven time and again — the systems work!

In 2015, I achieved my goal of having $2.8 million in cash and retired from the real estate industry. Now, I work 25 hours a week at The CORE Training as head of the real estate division, which gives me the ability to help agents like you bring more joy and profitability into their career. My passion is "paying it forward" and teaching you the steps that our CORE real estate students before you have used to explode their businesses while reducing their time spent at work.

We are creating millionaires every day. Why not join us?!

SECTION ONE: WHO WE ARE

About the Authors

Reeta Casey is a partner of The CORE Training, Inc., a national real estate coaching company. She credits Rick Ruby as the mentor who has had the biggest impact on her life by teaching her the systems and structure for a successful business.

By following The CORE's systems, Reeta built a profitable real estate business that she was able to sell in 2005. After selling her company, Reeta became the founding broker for Stockworth Realty Group, a boutique real estate company dedicated to the luxury market in central Florida. Her clientele included owners of lakefront and luxury homes, corporate relocation accounts, and professional athletes. Reeta's customer service systems resulted in long-term relationships with her clients, and even now after retiring from real estate, she continues to receive leads that she refers to her team.

Reeta Casey: A snapshot
- Bachelor of science in economics
- Licensed real estate professional for 27 years
- Consistently ranked in the Top 100 Real Estate Professionals in Orlando, FL
- $2.8 million in cash assets
- 20-year breast cancer survivor

Rick Ruby is the majority partner of The CORE Training, Inc. He keeps current in the lending market by running four Summit Funding branch offices. He has his best financial year ever every year due to his high level of commitment to playing BIG in everything he does.

Rick and Reeta met 16 years ago through another coaching company and became friends and colleagues. In 2001, they partnered with Todd Scrima and their operations manager, Britt Ruby, to start The CORE Training, Inc.

Rick Ruby & The CORE Training, Inc.: A snapshot

- The #1 mortgage coaching company in America
- 32 coaches personally coaching more than 350 members in Level 3 coaching
- Thousands of others in our 12 Steps to Double Your Income, Next 24, and Level 1.5 coaching programs
- Unmatched results: In the last five years, the average student began the program with $244,000 in personal income and graduated two years later with a net of over $512,000.

We share all of these facts to bring credibility to who we are and what we do, as well as to give you confidence in our programs and processes.

We believe you can learn the most from the people who have achieved the results you want. Your next step is to put our proven tactics into practice.

How to Read and Execute This Book

Consider this book to be a manual for building your profitable business. First, read the entire book to understand the overview of the model. Next, start from the beginning and read one chapter per day. During this phase, focus on mastering the steps outlined in each chapter.

In order to build a sustainable model, implement the tactics in the homework sections. By taking action, you will start building a business that produces $30 million in real estate sales. This structure should yield about $350,000 in net income (depending on splits and commission percentages earned).

We've also included graphs and templates to accompany our explanations and personal stories to help you easily understand and implement changes in your business.

We learn in four ways: By seeing, hearing, feeling/moving, and repetition until a habit is formed. Because we learn in different ways, we recommend you do the following activities to fully maximize your learning experience:

1. For one year, when you first wake up, read this book 15 minutes per day.
2. Do the homework assigned in every chapter.
3. Go The CORE website www.thecoretraining.com and sign up for one our webinars.

4. Follow us on the following social media for real estate tips:

>   Facebook: facebook.com/TheCoreRE
>   Twitter: @TheCoreRE
>   Linkedin: Reeta Casey

Following the processes outlined in this book will change how you run your business and live your life. To truly absorb the information in this book, we encourage you to enroll in one of The CORE coaching programs. We are committed to helping real estate agents like you, and coaching is our passion. We want to be your COACH!

Reeta Casey: Why I Wrote This Book

Our industry is one of the most exciting and opportunistic businesses in the world. Where else can you have an unlimited income, meet people from all walks of life, and build wonderful relationships? After 27 years, I still love the real estate business and feel compelled to share with my fellow agents the systems and structure to build a profitable and sustainable business. I am blessed to have had wonderful teachers and a few great mentors. My goal is to leave a positive mark on my industry through coaching real estate agents who are energetic, committed, and passionate about their clients on how to build a profitable business. I know that if you implement The CORE systems and structure, you will thrive in sales and build financial freedom.

Seventeen years ago I met my mentor, Rick Ruby, and his impact on my business and my life has been monumental. Through his guidance, I learned how to evolve my mindset from a real estate salesperson to a business person in the real estate industry. This may sound like a simple change, but it was HUGE! It was a complete mindset shift that allowed me to be coachable and accountable. This change created the ability for me to sell my real estate practice, set up a boutique real estate company, and now step out of the daily grind. By retiring from actively selling, I am able to share with you the critical steps of how to build a practice that creates wealth and a more balanced life.

One of our first struggles is the mentality created by the label "independent agent." This label gives us a false sense that we can do "whatever we want, whenever we want," which actually prevents us from being successful. Only through structure, systems, and accountability can we build a real estate practice that creates freedom in our lives. By building a team, we can consistently serve our clients' interests at the highest level while reducing our hours. By keeping track of our numbers, we learn exactly what we need to do next to grow our business, whether it be lead generation, cutting costs, or raising our average sales price. The numbers do not lie, so we must complete CORE forms monthly to truly understand how our business flows.

Many of the trainers at other real estate coaching companies have not been actively selling for many years; therefore, the information they provide you may be secondhand or even outdated. At The CORE, our coaches are <u>active</u> salespeople and our members are coached by agents who have achieved more than them in the areas of sales or cash net worth.

Thanks to Rick's tenacious coaching, I have attained wealth goals beyond what I ever dreamed. He has looked at my forms every month for the last 15 years. Yes, it was painful at times, but NO WAY would I trade the accountability and the stress for the success of hitting my financial goals. Now I can retire from actively selling and concentrate on helping great agents like you achieve your dreams and goals. I still receive business from the relationships I cultivated through my years as an agent, and I refer to my amazing real estate partner. She is a student herself because she is committed to serving our clients at the highest level.

Thanks to The CORE, I will always think BIG and have the opportunity to help you have a fun and profitable career.

Rick Ruby:
Why You Should Listen to Me

I've been a lender for 32 years and in the coaching business for 21, and I've been dealing with real estate agents my whole career. I've been super frustrated that most of the real estate agents that I deal with are broke and never seem to get ahead. I'll tell you a story.

An agent from the past
A real estate agent who I had done business with 15 years ago called me two weeks ago to catch up. He's a fabulous guy, about 50 years old. He saw me online, saw how big I was, and called to reconnect. I asked him how he was doing. He'd just gotten divorced and was still doing $10 million a year in production, just like 15 years ago. He's had no growth in his business. That's what frustrates me about real estate agents.

Striving for constant growth
I live my life on a mission for growth in every area of my life. So, everything that I do is about finding a new teacher, implementing a new system, and creating a different vision for my life and myself. That's what I'm about and what my business is about.

My life is based on the movie *Pay It Forward,* which is about a kid that tries to change the planet by helping a few people. Then those people help a few people, and it creates a domino effect. So in the coaching business, I am helping other people become more successful, and then I want them to go teach other people.

My business is based on two books. *Raving Fans* by Ken Blanchard and Sheldon Bowles is my favorite. It's a book about how to create a world-class experience, how to take great care of people, and how to create an experience that is fun. Buying a house and getting a mortgage is not fun, but we have to make it fun. The other book is called *The E-Myth* by Michael Gerber, and it teaches you how to go from an entrepreneur, where you do everything, to a business person, where you do almost nothing. I love that concept because being a great real estate agent is all consuming.

How Reeta and Rick got started
I've been a coach with Reeta now for 21 years since we were both with By Referral Only with Joe Stumpf, and we've had a lot of fun together. When I started coaching her, I realized that real estate agents have no concept of preparing a Profit & Loss statement or doing a personal budgeting system. So I designed a system to teach real estate agents how to be business people.

Make more money in fewer hours
So that's why agents should listen to me. I have some great tactics and great systems. I treat money tactically, not emotionally. That is a big thing for people to learn. If they follow me, they'll make a lot of money, save a lot of money, and work a lot fewer hours. If they don't follow me, they'll be like that guy that called me two weeks ago. In 15 years, they'll have the same business they have now, they'll struggle with the IRS, and they'll struggle with their life and their marriage.

If you want the same life in 15 years that you have now, keep doing what you are currently doing. You want a great life? Follow me.

Reeta's Story

In 1977, I received my degree in economics from the University of Tennessee at Knoxville. I knew I wanted to study business, but did not know exactly what career path I would take. I leaned towards economics, especially since it required the least amount of accounting classes. I was not sure how this degree would help me in business or life, but it gave me a structure of how to think through all types of situations and challenges.

After college, I floundered from job to job until I found my way into the restaurant business. My first position as a general manager was in Winter Park, Florida. I loved running this establishment. My staff and I grew the business by meeting local patrons and building relationships with them. The joy for me was facing new challenges daily and not being tied down to a desk doing paperwork. In addition, I was driven by the challenge of managing employees and holding my staff accountable to the standards and service specs of the brand. I was also held accountable for the inventory counts and generating a monthly Profit & Loss statement to make sure our results yielded a profit.

For seven years I worked in the restaurant industry. It was brutal, with my weekly hours over eighty, coupled with the night shifts starting at 4 p.m. and ending at 2 a.m. Finally, the late nights and early mornings made me realize I had to make a career change in order to live longer. The blessing for me is that the restaurant business led me to my husband, Pat, who was also in the business, but handled the environment better than I did. In 1983 we were married, and that was the end of that career. Now was the time for new opportunities.

I found my way into real estate during the home buying process. Pat and I had moved to Newburyport, Massachusetts and began our first-time buying search. Since we did not know a real estate agent, I walked into a local office. I was assigned the agent on floor duty to assist me with my needs. I will never forget that cold winter day when we headed out to view homes. The car window on the passenger's side was broken and would not roll up all the way. The temperature was in the 20s, and the ashtray was overflowing. At that moment I said to myself, "I know I can do a better job helping people buy a home!" This was the start of a career that lasted twenty-seven years.

What's your story?
Do you remember why you decided to get into the real estate industry? Write down your story.

CORE CULTURE

Around here…
We believe in prospecting, prospecting, and more prospecting.

We believe in building a team to cater to your clients.

We believe in counting the money.

We believe in holding each other accountable in order to get out of our comfort zone and perform at our best every day.

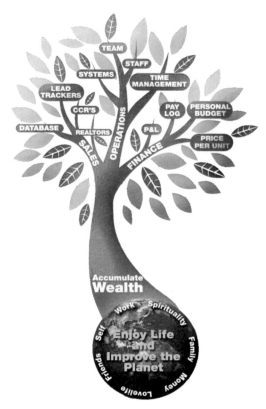

Rick Ruby on Accountability: The Heart of The CORE

When I go to the gym, I work out with a personal trainer. I show up and do what I'm told. He counts out loud to make sure I don't cheat the count. The other day he had me do pull ups. When he turned around to talk to somebody else, I went, "one, three, five, seven, nine, fifteen!" I got done by cheating, but the only person I cheated was myself. When you are held accountable, you're not able to cheat.

What accountability looks like at The CORE

Around here, we believe in holding people accountable by tracking information because numbers don't lie. I can tell ten people how to work a VIP list, but none of them are going to do it. I can make two people send me their VIP list and text me when they've made their calls, and they will do the list and they will make the calls.

We make a vision of where you're going in the next one year, three years, and five years. We set up tactics that you are going to implement every week, every month, every quarter, every year, and we evaluate how you are doing based on looking at your call sheets, pay logs, lead trackers, Profit & Loss, and personal budget.

The special ingredient

Accountability is at the heart of what we do. It's The CORE's special ingredient that separates us from other coaching that dumps a bunch of information. We provide tactics and watch that they get implemented. We make sure you make the count without cheating. That's really what accountability is.

Definitions

As you read this book, it will be important for you to know and understand the terminology of our industry and The CORE Training.

Lead: Anyone who wants to speak with you about real estate

Contract: Listing agreement, buyer contract, or a buyer representation agreement

CORE Forms:
- **Greatness Tracker:** A sales tracking tool
- **Lead Tracker:** Tracks every lead coming into the business and the source of the lead
- **Pay Log:** Tracks all the contracts (listings sold and sales agreements) in a given month, volume, income, etc.
- **Business Profit & Loss:** A form to track monthly expenses and income to see if your company made a profit for the month
- **Personal Budget:** Tracks every dollar you make and save in your personal life

Real Estate Agent: A salesperson

Real Estate Partner 1 (RP1): A team member that manages the database, your schedule, and all checklists for sellers and buyers

Real Estate Partner 2 (RP2): A team member that performs duties that require an active license, including taking listings, showing buyers, and answering specific real estate sales questions *(Consult your local Board as to the specific duties that require a license)*

Dialer: A telemarketer that sets appointments for you

Gross Commissions: The money generated from a closed sale calculated from the published selling percentage in your multiple listing contract

Net Commission: The money you actually receive after referral fees and company splits. It is the amount that shows up on your 1099 and you pay taxes on at the end of the year

Channel Account: An account such as a business, builder, or client who refers one closed deal per quarter

Happy Hour: A monthly social meeting at a restaurant the same day and time to network with your Top lists

Letter of the Heart (LOTH): A personal letter about you or your life experience. This letter is printed and mailed the first of every month to your personal friends, family, and clients who have completed a transaction with you.

Evidence of Success (EOS): A postcard that shows your success as a real estate salesperson. Examples might be "just listed" or "just sold" announcements. This is mailed to everyone including clients, friends, family, business people, and builders.

Big Ideas and Philosophies

Here are our basic beliefs that will help you understand the tactics in this book.

Three Ways to Make Money

1. **Your Time:** Limit to 40-50 hours per week
2. **Replication:** Team members do things you would have done. Delegate to keep yourself in your highest and best use, which is prospecting.
3. **Exponential:** You make money with very little or none of your time.

❖ If you are going to work 40-50 hours per week doing something, why not make and save a lot of money doing it?

❖ You are paid for the work you perform, not what you "think" or "feel" you are worth.

❖ Narcissism (thinking you are more important than anyone) is the enemy of learning and long-term success.

❖ Bigger Pile Principle: Learn from those who have the results you want.

❖ You MUST learn management and leadership skills to reach your potential in business.

CORE Culture

- Do the right thing
- Do your very best
- Show people you care

❖ Be a great student!

❖ Gratitude creates attitude

❖ Save 20% of your taxable income

❖ Business is 50% relationships and 50% execution; you must have both.

❖ If you don't have anyone working for you, you don't have a business. You have a JOB.

❖ Structure is the key to improve any business. The more structured you are, the more success you will have.

Who Fits This Career?

Real estate is a challenging sales career and perfectly suited for the person who is driven by creating his or her own income. If you want the opportunity to make an unlimited amount of money based on your results, along with getting up each day knowing you are responsible for the outcome, then jump on board!

These are the primary characteristics of a highly successful real estate agent:

→ You are self-motivated.

→ You love helping people.

→ You are enthusiastic and passionate about selling.

→ You are driven to create unlimited income.

→ You are coachable!

Rick Ruby: Using The CORE Test to Measure Your Business

The CORE Test measures your current business model and covers three areas: sales, operations, and life.

The sales test asks questions about sales tactics like, "Do I talk to 60 people a week? Do I send a mailer to my database every month? Do I send 10 thank you cards every week?"

The operations test asks about your operations. "Do I work off of a printed daily schedule? Does someone else manage my emails and texting?" Those are things that you need to do. Remember the lessons from the book *Raving Fans* on creating a world-class experience and *The E-Myth* on going from technician to business person. The operations test will help you make those transitions in your business.

You should do the test twice a year and see where your score is. Use this test to determine what areas of your business need improvement and what systems need to be implemented. Every time you do the test, you should implement one or two more things you can then knock off the list.

We've included the test in here and I want you to stop right now and take it.

Take the Test

Take a few minutes to complete The CORE Test on the next few pages. Circle "Yes" if something happens every time. If you have to pause and think about the answer, then circle "No."

I. CORE SALES TEST

Please
Circle

1. I average $3-15 million monthly as a Lender or 5-15 sides at $7,500 as a Realtor.   Yes No
2. I see 15 people face to face every week.   Yes No
3. I send 10 thank you cards every week.   Yes No
4. I have 5 Break Breads with influential people every week.   Yes No
5. I talk to 60 people every week.   Yes No
6. I have a 10-person whale list that I work weekly.   Yes No
7. I have a Top 50 VIP list, and I call 12 per week.   Yes No
8. I mail to my database of at least 400 contacts once every month.   Yes No
9. I call all past clients to do annual reviews four years back.   Yes No
10. I have a Top 50 Past Clients list, and I call 12 per week.   Yes No
11. I generate 40 leads per month.   Yes No
12. I perform Tuesday update calls for all my clients and referral sources every week.   Yes No
13. I send 1,000 video emails per month.   Yes No
14. I have two channel accounts that send me 10 deals each per year.   Yes No
15. I listen to at least two training CDs every month.   Yes No
16. I do a Happy Hour every month.   Yes No
17. I spend four hours per day selling and prospecting for new business.   Yes No
18. I survey every client and receive a minimum score of 8 out of 10 on 90% of my surveys.   Yes No
19. I hold or attend one group training or seminar every month.   Yes No
20. I send birthday cards to my Top 50 VIPs and Top 50 Past Clients.   Yes No

Total possible "Yes" Scores for this Section: 20   Your Score _____

Score 17 – 20: You are doing the work and your income should be $250,000 – $1 million.

Score 12 – 16: You are on your way and your income should be $125,000 – $300,000.

Score under 12: You probably should find a new job.

II. CORE Management & Organization Test

Please Circle

1.	My yearly and 5 year goals are laminated and in the back of my Blue Beast.	Yes No
2.	I have a team outing every month.	Yes No
3.	I have a current flowchart that is enlarged, framed, and hanging on the wall.	Yes No
4.	I have a daily team meeting with checklists.	Yes No
5.	I have detailed job descriptions and contracts for each team member's position.	Yes No
6.	My team vision and mission are enlarged, framed, and hanging on the wall.	Yes No
7.	I have attended Rapport Leadership 1.	Yes No
8.	My assistant or LP1/RP1 handle all my scheduling.	Yes No
9.	I have a welcome board for all guests.	Yes No
10.	I have a structure pipeline meeting every week.	Yes No
11.	I have visited the offices of two CORE coaches.	Yes No
12.	I do the Wheel of Life with my team every year and help them set their goals.	Yes No
13.	I do a performance review with all my employees semi-annually.	Yes No
14.	I have an operations manual for all systems.	Yes No
15.	My voicemail lists my call back times.	Yes No
16.	I list only one phone number on all my materials (no cell).	Yes No
17.	My Day-at-a-Glance is printed and on my desk before I arrive every morning and at the end of the day.	Yes No
18.	My desk has a phone, computer, my Blue Beast and only one file on it at a time.	Yes No
19.	My work appearance is extremely professional. That includes my clothing, shoes, hair, and overall grooming.	Yes No
20.	My LP1/RP1 handle all my emails.	Yes No

Total possible "Yes" Scores for this Section: 20   Your Score: _____

Score 17-20: Awesome – You are building a great, long-term profitable business. You are working under 40 hours per week.

Score 12-15: Medium Stress – You are working 45-70 hours per week and don't have much fun. Be a better student.

Score under 12: Havoc and a lot of stress. Check out a new career – you will BURN OUT.

III. CORE Money & Life Test

Please Circle

1. I save 20% of Column 5 on my Personal Budget every month.   Yes No
2. I fill out a budget every month.   Yes No
3. I give at least 5% of my taxable income to causes I believe in.   Yes No
4. I have a Trust and update it yearly.   Yes No
5. I own at least two properties: my primary and a secondary or rental.   Yes No
6. My cash net worth is at $2 million.   Yes No
7. I have $1 million of equity in my properties.   Yes No
8. I go on 3 weeks of vacation every year.   Yes No
9. I take 3 weekends per month off for myself and family enjoyment.   Yes No
10. I perform 10 hours of community service per year.   Yes No
11. I have a weekly spiritual practice like church, small group, or meditating.   Yes No
12. I have a fixed mortgage of 70% or less for all my Real Estate.   Yes No
13. I carry zero debt except for my mortgage.   Yes No
14. I maintain three months of my survival # at all times.   Yes No
15. I carry 5-10 times my yearly income in fixed term life insurance.   Yes No
16. I have a least one date with my significant other every week.   Yes No
17. People around me can tell that I love what I do for a living.   Yes No
18. My life and business are based on the movie *Pay it Forward*.   Yes No
19. I spend at least three hours a week pursuing my hobbies.   Yes No
20. I am involved in a charity organization.   Yes No

Total possible "Yes" Scores for this Section: 20   Your Score: _____

Score 16-20: You have arrived! Kick back and enjoy the ride – how sweet it is! ☺

Score 12-15: You are on your way. Have fun and lighten up – teach others and you will grow from it.

Score 9-11: Knuckle down, step it up and stay the course. Be a better student!

Score under 9: Danger – Danger – Danger

Total possible "Yes" Scores for all 3 Sections: 60

Your total Score: _____ ÷ .60

= Total %: _____

III. Extra Credit List

Please Circle

1.	I chase four expired listings or two Superstar Realtors every week.	Yes No
2.	I have seen the movie *Door to Door* three times.	Yes No
3.	I have attended Rapport Leadership 2.	Yes No
4.	I have attended Rapport Leadership "Power Communications."	Yes No
5.	I have watched the movies: *Hoosiers, Remember the Titans, Coach Carter.*	Yes No
6.	I review the personal budgets of all my team members every month.	Yes No
7.	My business is run by the three principles of the book *Raving Fans.*	Yes No
8.	My car is clean inside and out at all times.	Yes No
9.	My closet is organized and neat.	Yes No
10.	I participate on two Open Line Calls per month.	Yes No
11.	I have one business and one personal credit card.	Yes No
12.	I send a LOTH every month.	Yes No
13.	I take 30 minutes a day and three hours per week for myself.	Yes No
14.	My people rate working for our company at a 9.	Yes No
15.	I work 40 hours or less per week.	Yes No

Total possible "yes" scores for this section: 15   Your score: _____

Reeta's Personal Journey to Balance

Was The CORE Test a wake-up call for you?

I will never forget my wake-up call and how it changed the direction of my business and life.

I remember that Friday vividly. I was leaving my home to open up a property I had for sale. The house was located in Bay Hill Village and belonged to PGA Golfer Payne Stewart and his wife, Tracy. This was our first showing, and I was excited to represent them.
As I was leaving my home to drive over, I had an incredibly sharp pain that caused me to double over and see stars. Wow! I had never experienced anything like that before and realized I needed to get to an emergency room — IMMEDIATELY!! What a crazy week with my annual mammogram, a full real estate calendar, and now this emergency.

On Monday, my doctor (who was also my client) called and let me know I would be okay as far as the issue that had sent me to the hospital. I had a cyst burst, and the internal bleeding is what had caused the pain; however, he needed for Pat and I to come into his office to discuss the results of my mammogram. This was a huge shock..

We went to my physician's office, where he proceeded to tell me I had something suspicious show up on my mammogram. My next step in the process was to have a needle wire biopsy to determine if I had breast cancer. The following week, Pat and I went to the hospital to have the procedure.

After the biopsy, my surgeon came into the recovery room to give Pat and I the results. The tissue had tested positive for breast cancer. It was time for me to move forward to fix it rather than stay in a place of self-pity; therefore, my immediate response was, "What is the next step?"

At first, I thought I would take a few weeks off to heal. This was not realistic, so Pat, my surgeon, and I came up with a plan together to get Reeta healthy. Over the next month, I immersed myself in holistic treatments, followed by a scheduled mastectomy 30 days later. Needless to say, this was a life-changing event that took a little more time to heal from physically and emotionally. Yes, this experience caused me to re-evaluate my life.

During my recovery, I came to the realization that I loved my career in real estate, and, fortunately, I had created clients that trusted and referred me. What a relief to have business coming in while I was focused on my recovery. Also, I knew I had to come up with a plan to cut my hours and spend more time with my family, and myself. That's when I created a new vision for my team.

Once I recovered and was fully back in the business, I decided to share my new vision with my team. I remember sharing the details of the changes we were going to make in the business. At the time, I had three team members plus myself, and I was so excited to share our new direction.

I felt so good about our future, but was shocked to find that over the course of the next four months, everyone on the team quit! At first I asked myself, "Is this really happening to me?" I had just survived breast cancer and was on the road to recovery, and now on top of everything else, I had a real estate team that was falling apart. When the day came that the last person left the team, I went home and told Pat I needed a drink. He offered me a lovely glass of wine, but I said, "No, tonight I will take a shot of whiskey, please."

After my 24-hour pity party, I got fired up and decided to start building a new team that would help me create my real estate business and bring my vision to life. Looking back, I realized that when we change our vision, we have to be prepared to let go of the people that do not share the same goals. What I learned is that if we are open to change, nature will support us in our new direction by removing the obstacles blocking us from achieving them.

I knew I was on the right path to restructure my business. What I did not know is who was going to help me get there. Rick Ruby was my life line when he decided to start a new coaching company. How thrilled I was to be a part of this exciting new venture to change both the lending and real estate industries. What I did not know was how life-changing it would be.

This life lesson was the wake-up call I needed to live the rest of my life from a place of gratitude. I am forever grateful to God for every day of my life, for Pat's love and support, and for my family and friends who offer me continuous love and support.

My prayer for you is to wake up and re-evaluate where you are. Are you working too many hours? Are you spending quality time with your family? Are you stressing over money? If you answered "yes" to any of these questions, then it is time to surrender and become coachable. Implement The CORE systems and transform your business to one that consistently nets you a profit every month. Get excited by the money you save and the hours you cut out of your schedule. Become a real estate business person NOW!

SECTION TWO:
PROSPECT,
PROSPECT,
PROSPECT

RICK RUBY: MOVING PAST THE FEAR OF PROSPECTING

The only two driving forces that make everyone do what they do is love and fear. Fear is a gigantic force in all human beings. We're all afraid. I'm afraid every time I go on stage before I give a talk. I'm afraid of writing this book that you're not going to find my information credible. Sometimes I'm just afraid of the unknown. So, fear is a giant, driving force.

Conscious and subconscious fear

People have a fear of prospecting because they fear the unknown or they fear rejection. They even fear being successful, maybe without realizing it. Why would people be afraid of success? Well, what do many people do with a lot of money? Many people with a lot of money do bad things. We all see that, right? Politicians acting up, rich businessmen acting a fool, movie stars committing suicide. We see a lot of rich people acting up, and a lot of us are subconsciously afraid that if we made all of these sales calls and made all of this money that we might act up. So when it comes to prospecting, there are both conscious and subconscious fears that you have to deal with. When you beat the fear, you will make a lot of money.

Reframing fear into love

What I do is draw a line down a piece of paper. When things come up, I decide whether I frame it as a loving thing or a fearful thing. When you bring up the word "prospecting," most people put it in the fear side. Let me tell you how to reframe your fear into love.

You reframe fear by saying things like this: "I love prospecting because it gives me an opportunity to meet and help new people and make more money."

That's how you reframe your fear.

Take another example: Building a team. People have a great fear of building a team. It's the same thing. Reframe it by telling yourself, "I love building my team because it creates more jobs and gives me the ability to help more clients and do what I do really, really well."

Moving past rejection

Fear of prospecting means that you are going to get rejected. Period. I'm loud, aggressive, and direct. So I'm going to get rejected 70% of the time. I know from my 35 years in sales that out of every ten people I approach, seven will struggle with me. But what I also know, because I have developed my character and leadership skills over the last ten years, that the personalities that don't like me up front, if they get to know me, they appreciate me and respect me. I'm a good person. I'm honest. I have a big heart. I'm very generous. These are things that people don't know about me until they look behind the curtain. To get them to look behind the curtain, I have to follow up. I call on somebody, and then I set up a system to contact them seven times after the initial contact.

When you're prospecting, you've got to look at it like you're playing basketball or playing Rummy or Uno. It's a game. They win or you win. The key is, you're going to win half the time. If you're really good, you figure out how to win 60 to 80% of the time. I'll tell you this, if a guy asks enough girls out, they're going to say yes!

Uncover the objection to make the sale

Now listen, if I ask somebody to do business with me and they say, "No," my response is: "Why not?" I want to know the objection so I can overcome it. You have to uncover the objection to make a sale.

Agent: "Why don't you want to buy this house?"

Buyer: "It's got green wallpaper."

That objection is very easy to overcome. We can change the wallpaper!

You've got to get over the fear of prospecting, or you're just going to be broke. That's the bottom line. Don't call on anybody, be broke. Call on people, be rich. Is it that simple? Yes!

Which do you think I chose?

HOW TO PROSPECT

Where does business come from?

Prospecting is the most dreaded activity by salespeople, but the most critical to master in order to excel in creating leads for your business. If you truly want to have a profitable career in real estate, then it is your responsibility to contact people and ask who needs help with buying or selling real estate. If we truly love helping people, we need to contact them.

In a perfect world, your sales should break down into the following categories by percentage:

- **25% – VIPs and Top 50 Past Clients**
  These are your favorite people and your favorite past clients

- **25% – Database**
  This is the remaining list of family, friends, and those who have completed a transaction with you

- **25% – Business People**
  These are contacts in your community who have a database of potential customers in need of real estate help

- **25% – Other**
  This category is made up of leads from sign calls, advertisements, the Internet, builders, etc.

The Perfect Model

The Perfect Model is designed to build a long-term, sustainable business based on relationships. While Internet leads and cold leads are short-term cotton candy, relationships are the key to longevity and profitability. And besides, why recreate new business every day when you could be working consistent leads?

How do you create good relationships in the first place? This starts with consistent networking through what we call "Green Time" — or prospecting time — during which you contact and build on your relationships with past clients, business people, and new leads. This means you must get out of your office and sell the product — YOU. The success formula is to set aside two hours per day specifically to prospect. This one activity is the key to changing your real estate business.

Seven Pillars of Business

At The CORE, we have seven groups of people you can prospect for business:

Pillar #1 - Current Client Referrals (CCR): There is no better time to ask for a referral than when your clients are going through the process. During that time, they are acutely aware of other people who are talking about real estate. This awareness stems from a segment of the brain called the Reticular Activator.

Pillar #2 - Past Clients (PC): People who have been through a transaction with you before and are ready to buy or sell again.

Pillar #3 - Past Client Referrals (PCR): These are leads from your past clients. This type of lead is the highest compliment you can receive because they have experienced your service and now trust you to help one of their friends, family, and coworkers enjoy the same service.

Pillar #4 - Personal Friends (PF): Your sphere of influence

Pillar #5 - Advertisements (AD): Cold leads from the Internet, a sign call, an open house, a print ad, or any other form of marketing not attached to a relationship

Pillar #6 - Business People (BP): These people are the best untapped source of referrals. Business people also prospect for new leads and are looking for a professional, trustworthy real estate agent to send their business.

Pillar #7 - Builders: These can include individuals or corporate home builders. Often they have their own on-site agents, but building relationships with them and their on-site sales team can have profitable results for you down the road.

Tracking your business

The image below is from the Lead Tracker form (in The Blue Beast). The Lead Tracker breaks down the source of your leads and your closing percentage. By taking a hard look at your incoming business, you will know where you need to spend more time prospecting.

G										_____ x 20% = _____
									Total	
	CCR	PCR	PC	PF	RLTR	AD	BUS	BLDR	Month	Total Written Transactions
L										_____ / _____ Listings / Buyers
T										Transactions _____ div. by Leads _____ = Closing % _____

L = Leads   T = Transactions   G = Goal
Number of circled Hot Leads at the end of the month: _____

The Perfect Model

Sales Mindset

Your mindset is critical to successful prospecting.

My first question to you is: Do you love helping people buy and sell real estate?

If your answer is yes, then the next question is: Are you the best person to help someone with their real estate transaction?

Again if your answer is, "Yes!", then it is your obligation to talk to at least ten people per day and find out if they know someone who needs your help. When you consistently ask if they need real estate help, then you increase the percentage that you will find a new customer. When you get a no, then realize they are only saying "not now." You are closer to finding the next person who will say yes. Remember, you are in charge of finding people who are in need of your service, and the more people you ask, the more opportunities you will create to find new clients.

For some reason, there are agents who try to avoid rejection, but that is impossible. Think about prospecting like fishing. You must bait the hook and cast the line into the water before you can even hope for a bite. If a fisherman only wet a hook when he knew he was guaranteed to catch a fish, then no one would even attempt it.

Prospecting is not personal. It's business. And it's the most critical part of our business. Having ten great conversations a day is a doable task, and when done consistently, it will dramatically improve your results. Get started today, and remember, you owe it to the buying or selling public to find those who need help and to be there for them.

Be careful! Most agents will go on a sales call and use the word "I" more than any other word by far. This is a problem. You want to capture interest and get people to say Wow! You do that by asking questions and having them talk. If you really care about the person in front of you, then make a positive impression.

Here are a few steps to get you started:
1. **Say something positive.**
2. **Give them your elevator speech (more on this later).**
3. **Be passionate about what you do.**
4. **Ask for their help.**

 Take the Sales Mindset Quiz
Before you start prospecting, consider the following questions about your sales mindset.

Question #1: What do you do for a living?

Question #2: What is your product?

Question #3: What service do you offer?

Question #4: Who is your client?

THE ROADMAP TO A PROFITABLE $30 MILLION REAL ESTATE BUSINESS

Answers:

#1 – You are a salesperson.

#2 – You are the product.

#3 – You assist clients who are buying or selling real estate.

#4 – Your clients are qualified builders, business people, friends, family, and co-workers who are ready to purchase or sell their real estate asset.

Reeta Casey: Organized Database

Your organized database is the gold mine of your business. This group should be made up of current client referrals (CCR), past clients (PC), past client referrals (PCRs), and personal friends (PF).

Early in my career, I realized that my database was a growing and changing pool of relationships. During my time at another coaching company, I learned how important referrals are to the growth of my business. In order to create a business structure that produces consistent leads, I needed to continually deepen my relationships. To do that, I had to add systems of communication.

Many people ask me, how did I get my database started? First, I selected a software system to input my contacts so that I could create systems. There are several choices of software on the market today, so find one that meets your needs.

For me it was important to have one that was cloud based so I could access it via mobile device. I used an online CRM because it also gave me the team component I needed. We could type notes into the client contact, and whenever a client called, anyone on the team could pull up the notes and continue the conversation. This developed trust between my team members and our clients since the clients did not have to always talk to me to get updates about their transaction. Also, it allowed us to create checklists with action steps delegated to specific team members with a deadline. All this happened with a simple press of the "launch" button.

To illustrate the importance of having a replicable WOW experience, do you think McDonald's has detailed guest experience checklists and procedures? Of course! And they want to make sure that whether you are dining at their store in Orlando or San Diego, you have the same quality food and service. By running your real estate practice this way, you will replicate a memorable experience for every client, and that will result in consistent referrals.

When CORE Coach Kendra Cooke learned the benefits of an organized database and applied them to her business, it made all the difference in the world and her business exploded! Read her story on the next page.

SUCCESS STORY: KENDRA COOKE

The database. I've heard it called my "sphere of influence," my "money maker," my "contacts," and so many other things over the years, but I never knew why I needed one until I joined The CORE. I couldn't figure out why I was working so hard and never had any money left over at the end of the month until I audited my business and realized I was spending all my resources, both time and money, on people who didn't know me or trust me. How crazy was that?! I was closing 10 to 12 deals per month and doing a fairly good job during the transaction, but never realized that group of people liked me and trusted me, and they might have a friend that could use my services, too.

Rather than continue down the path of spending 80% of my commissions on advertisements, shopping carts, mailers and anything else I could find, I went back to my old files, built a database of my old clients, and started to spend money on them. I sent mailers, calendars, and had small client parties that I could afford. It gave me a way to ask them for referrals.

Fast forward nine years, and in 2014, more than 90% of our business came from our database and VIPs. I truly run a relationship business that provides me great leads on a monthly basis, and I am now keeping more than 45% of my profits for ME! Stop where you are in your business today and put together your database and watch your leads roll in.

— **Kendra Cooke**, *founding member of Cooke Realty Partners*

So have I convinced you to get a database software system and start the organizing process?

Organizing your database

If you want to avoid the extreme highs and lows of real estate, you must have systems and structure in your business. We organize the database into two categories modeled after the Seven Pillars of Business: Clients and Leads.

Clients will include both those who have been through a transaction with you and those whom you personally know. This category includes past clients, current clients, friends and family.

Leads will include people you have met through business networking, builders, etc., that refer you, but have not closed a transaction with you.

This easy method of organizing our contacts will give you the opportunity to continue developing relationships based on systematic communications.

Mail – Call – Visit

When building relationships, it is important to interact with people via different methods of communication. At The CORE, we teach a three-step approach: Mail, Call, Visit.

Mail

In today's world, handwritten notes and letters are a lost art. Everyone loves to receive personal correspondence as it shows the person that you care because you took the time to write and mail the communication. This is an effective way to make a great impression on someone.

Call

Calling your clients is an impactful way to stay in touch. Are you avoiding the phone because you do not know what to say? Focus on making your clients feel important by asking questions about themselves. Remember that for your clients, a "great" phone call is one in which they spend the majority of the time talking about what is going on in their life. Think of yourself as an interviewer focused on updating yourself on the client and their family. A perfect script to use for this is the FORD script:

FORD Script

Family – People love to talk about their kids and immediate family.

Occupation – You should know where your clients work. The answers to these questions can open up possible referral accounts, which we will discuss later in this book.

Recreation – What they do for fun? What are their hobbies? Any new hobbies?
Dreams – Get to know what they are passionate about or what drives them so you can support them.

FORD in Action
Call 10 people in your database every day for one week and use the FORD script.

Visit

Visiting a client at work or at their home deepens your relationship with them. When you engage with someone face to face, it creates a more personal interaction, giving them a sense of appreciation. You go from being an agent who is selling your services to a person who cares about them. This visit fulfills your promise that you will stay in touch with them even after the sale.

This relationship goes even deeper and becomes more impactful when you share food or drink with your client. Our business relationship develops into a friendship when we "break bread" with our clients.

Face to Face
Schedule to meet face to face this week with five people who are current clients, past clients, past client referrals, or friends.

Four Steps to Professional Sales

Whether you are working with a seller, a buyer, or a referral account, there are four major steps to any sale:

Step 1 – Initial Contact: You reached out and made an appointment.

Step 2 – Rapport: They met you, like you, like what you offer, or both.

Step 3 – Close: They sign a listing or buyer agreement, or a sales contract with you, and then they send you a lead.

Step 4 – Follow Up: Systematic contact and meetings to stay connected and serving the client.

When The CORE does presentations around the country, we ask our audiences to rate themselves on those four skill areas to determine their sales strengths and weaknesses. Of those polled, we have learned that:

- More than 80% of all salespeople say they are best at rapport building.
- Less than 3% say they are best at initial contact/making lots of calls to set up meetings.

WOW! We can draw two quick conclusions from this feedback:
1. People like other people, so almost anyone can develop rapport.
2. The salesperson who makes the most sales calls wins.

Our students across the nation have proven these facts over and over again. When they dedicate two hours a day to dialing (what we refer to as Green Time), their results explode. Why? The more people you talk to a week, the more appointments you'll set. So, if you're talking to 60 people a week, you will drastically increase the number of appointments you set. From there, our students have seen their listings and sales double and triple. This all comes down to a dramatically higher income. Your personality type does not matter here; we coach people of all types. However, it is the ones that prospect without fail and implement The CORE plan that create unlimited potential.

Green Time

Commit to Green Time dialing for two hours per day for one week. Time block this and stick to it!

Target Marketing: Geographic Farm

I learned during my career that by implementing systems to the buying and selling processes, every client had a "WOW" experience. This resulted in a consistent stream of referrals. However, I still needed to add other sources of leads to increase my volume. One of the new systems we started was target marketing to a **geographic farm**, which was critical to my team's growth.

Why implement a geographic farm?

I built my real estate business in southwest Orlando, specifically the Dr. Phillips/Windermere area. Every piece of marketing that I created, tested, and implemented was for the residents of this particular area of central Florida. The consistency of my communication in a concentrated area meant that even when a particular marketing idea was a flop, I still gained name recognition in that area.

Don't be afraid to try something new

One of my craziest ideas was in 1993 when I mailed out expired letters stuffed inside a red tube with a cap and white thread that made it look like a stick of dynamite. I remember the day I got a call from the sheriff's department because a resident was scared to open it! In the end, it was fun testing different ideas as I searched out techniques that no one else was using. All the while, the residents of southwest Orlando saw my name or face all over the area, which continually boosted leads.

How to work a geographic farm

In today's competitive real estate environment, The CORE recommends a geographic farm made up of at least 1,000 rooftops. You will send out an "evidence of success" postcard monthly to market the properties you have listed or sold in that targeted area. In addition, you should bullet point the benefits of hiring your services, along with a call to action. If you do not have a property to market in that area, do a real estate market update on recent sales that include MLS statistics on the neighborhood. The key is repetitive communication: Mail consistently in order to create opportunities for people to recognize and remember you. Just the fact that you are organized enough to send mail consistently will separate you from your competition.

Seize opportunities for face-to-face meetings

When you put a house on the market in your geographic farm, maximize the opportunity by holding a preview of the property for the neighbors before it goes on the market. This will give you an opportunity to have a face-to-face interaction with potential new sellers in your geographic farm area.

Maximize results with structures and time

It takes a commitment to market monthly to get the maximum results. Too many times, my CORE students get frustrated when they do these activities for months and do not get results. This activity has a compounding effect, so stick with it. Remember, you are a real estate business person and in charge of selling your services. You MUST have a system to implement clear, consistent marketing messages to your targeted groups and deepen relationships to generate referrals.

Target Marketing: The Top Clubs

At The CORE, our clients generate between 25% and 50% of their business from people on their Top Lists. Our clients develop these lists from their database by selecting their favorite relationships. By executing the structured systems that we teach, our clients deepen these top tier relationships and build trust, and this leads to more referrals. What's more, these referrals tend to be at a higher price point, which goes to show the importance of working these lists effectively.

There are two lists:

❖ **The Top 50 VIPs**
> ➤ These are your family, friends, and influential business people and community members with whom you have a relationship. Think of your favorite people in your life.

❖ **The Top 50 Past Clients**
> ➤ These are the clients that you loved working with, who loved their experience with you, and would be highly likely to send you referrals.

Both of these lists are made up of people who know and trust us, and send their friends, family, and co-workers to us for their real estate needs. Start your lists now and continue to grow them until they reach 50 people each.

Working your Top Lists and your farm

Ensuring a structured system means getting it on your calendar. Here are the steps we recommend plotting out throughout the day, week, month, and year to consistently market to your farm and develop those relationships with your Top Lists:

- **Daily**
  - Spend two hours making prospecting calls to your lists (We will talk about who to call each day with "theme days" later in this book.)

- **Weekly**
  - Every Monday, send a video email to your clients with a real estate market update
  - Each week, target a different group (current clients, past clients, and business people)

- **Monthly**
  - Day 1: Send a Letter of the Heart to your database
  - Day 8: Mail a cheesy gift to your prospective business clients
  - Day 15: Mail an evidence of success postcard
  - Third Thursday: Happy Hour

- **Yearly**
  - Call the people on your Top lists the day before their wedding/relationship anniversary
  - For your Top Clubs, drop by their office with a cupcake on their birthday
  - Host an annual client party (This is a great way to say "thank you" to your clients and to enjoy and remember why you decided to go into real estate!)

Take a look at the marketing calendar on the next page. In November, you will sit down with a calendar like this and schedule your recurring events for the following year. At our November Summit, we set our business goals and marketing calendars so we are ready to implement January 1st.

Marketing Calendar

Take a moment to set up your marketing calendar for the next 12 months.

The CORE Marketing Calendar

SUNDAY	MONDAY	TUESDAY	WEDNESDAY	THURSDAY	FRIDAY	SATURDAY
		1 LOH (Letter of the Heart)	2	3	4	5
6	7 Videos	8 Mail "Cheesy Gift"	9	10	11	12
13	14 Videos	15 EOS (Evidence of Success)	16	17 HH (Happy Hour)	18	19
20	21 Videos	22	23	24	25	26
27	28 Videos	29	30			

53

Networking Events

In order for you to build the business people in your database and to develop great relationships, you need to get out of the office and meet other people in business. This will give you the chance to meet a variety of other folks in various businesses who can help you immediately or connect you later throughout your career.

A great formula filling your Greatness Tracker is to attend two events per month. To make it fun, take a friend and play off each other's competitive side with a prospecting game! The person who collects the most business cards within a certain period of time gets the other person to buy him or her a drink.

Before you head to an event, you'll want to prepare your "elevator speech." This is a prepared introduction about yourself when you only have a few minutes to make an impression on a stranger.

Example: *"Hi, my name is Reeta Casey, and I am a real estate agent with ABC Realty, serving the Windermere area. I pride myself on being a great communicator and expert negotiator. An ideal lead for me would be anyone looking to buy or sell real estate in either of those areas. If I could get your card, I would love to follow up with you in a day or two and see if we could schedule a time to talk to see if we could do some business together in the future."*

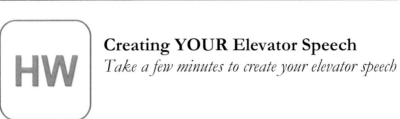

Creating YOUR Elevator Speech
Take a few minutes to create your elevator speech

1. Who are you?

   _____

2. What company are you with?

   _____

3. Where is your office located?

   _____

4. Your experience…be brief

   _____

   _____

5. What is your bait?
   a. _____
   b. _____
   c. _____

6. What is your need?

   _____

With the notes you made above, write your 20-30 second elevator speech, then memorize it and start using it!

Wow! Creating that was easy, and now you are ready at a moment's notice to precisely communicate what you do and whom you serve. This brings you a step closer to becoming a "business person." You will find that working with business people is not only fun, but profitable. Let's look at CORE coach, Allen Huggins, who has excelled in this category.

Building success through business relationships

When Allen Huggins, from Nashville, Tennessee, attended a Summit, he was netting $90,000. He wanted to join Level 3 coaching, but didn't meet the income requirements. Because of his unwavering enthusiasm and commitment, we decided to take a chance on him and accept him into our two-year coaching program.

Allen began watching his business grow, but after about 12 months, he hit a wall. He was filling up his Greatness Tracker, but did not have a substantial increase in his leads or transactions. He was so frustrated that he considered quitting. Then he had a call with his coach. They broke down who he was calling and what he was saying on those calls. When they examined his lead generating activities, they found that Allen was meeting with enough people, but his business partners were not referring him to new customers. It was time for him to "fire" some of his relationships and build new ones. Once Allen started meeting new people, he formed new business relationships and his leads exploded.

Now Allen has a strong referral business from professionals, which has resulted in raising his net profit by 60% and put him on track to net more than $500,000 in income. He is also working fewer hours, giving him more time with his family. Way to go, Allen!

Rick Ruby: The Greatness Tracker and the Blue Beast

What is the Blue Beast?

The Blue Beast is a tool that tracks all of your information from phone calls, your to-do list, your leads, commission, income, and personal budget. The first form to get started with is the phone log. Write down every incoming call. Next, mark every time you call that person. Keep that log for three months and call every contact seven times. That's the first place to get organized. Get away from sticky notes, get away from legal pads, and keep everything in the Blue Beast.

What is the Greatness Tracker?

The Greatness Tracker (see example on page 50) is an old-fashioned sales call sheet. It tracks how many people you talk to, people you've seen face to face, meetings you've been to, thank you cards you've sent, leads, and deals for a one-week period.

Yes, it may seem old-fashioned, but ask the greatest sales people on the planet, and you'll learn they've all been on a call sheet many times. I'm on a call sheet every day. Today, I have talked to 27 people on the phone and sent out 14 birthday and thank you cards. That's a lot of activity.

Phone calls are like reps at the gym

Most of you don't have enough activity because you don't track your activity. When you have a personal trainer, the trainer counts how many reps you did of each exercise. You don't just lift until you are tired. The trainer gives you a number and you shoot for it.

Every week, we want you to see 15 people face to face, including buyers, sellers, business people, or referral sources. We want you to break bread with five people and talk to 60 people. Now, that doesn't mean you dialed 60 telephone numbers and left voicemails. It means you have a conversation with 60 people.

The conversation sounds like this: "Hey, I want to be your real estate agent. I want to list your house. I want to help you find your dream house." Those are the three things you say. You say those three things to all clients all the time. That's the key to being a good salesperson.

The difference between amateur and professional
Call sheets are the difference between amateur and professional salespeople. You want to be an amateur? Be an amateur. You want to be a professional? Do a call sheet. The Greatness Tracker is a real estate agent's call sheet.

Greatness Tracker

		Mon	Tues	Wed	Thurs	Fri	Weekend	Week Total
Face	1							15
to	2							
Face	3							
Break	1							5
Bread	2							
Great	1							60
Phone	2							
Calls	3							
	4							
with leads	5							
referral partners	6							
past clients	7							
current clients	8							
	9							
	10							
Events								1 or 2
Hours Prospected								21
Thank You	1							10
Cards	2							
Leads								10
Deals								3

THE SALES APPOINTMENT

Dress for Success

Remember you sell for a living and the product is YOU. You need to dress as a trusted real estate advisor. People are selling or buying the largest personal investment of their lifetime, and your appearance is their first impression of you. Clients want to be proud of their agent, and they select you from not only your sales presentation, but your appearance.

For men, "professional" means wearing slacks and a suit jacket (or a nice button down shirt in the hotter months of the year). If you dress casually, such as in a golf shirt, you will give the impression that you take this business casually.

For women, remember that you are an executive, not a fashion diva. Stiletto heels and strappy sandals are tough when showing homes, especially new construction. Pack a pair of walking shoes, as I have ruined many an expensive pair when walking through dirt, mud, and construction zones.

For both men and women, remember that people are checking out every detail about you, from your nails and face, to your shoes and aromas. Be conscious to be manicured in every respect, and pack a travel pouch with cologne, a toothbrush, and toothpaste to freshen up during those long days.

Making a good impression extends to your car. You will spend time in your car driving your clients around, so be sure that your car is also a positive reflection of your organization. Do you remember my experience in Newburyport, Massachusetts, in the dead of winter? The passenger seat window would not roll all the way up and the ashtray was overflowing with cigarette ashes. As inexperienced with real estate as I was at the time, I told my husband that I could have done a better job. This is not the type of impression you want to leave with your clients!

Think – Feel – Know

Sales is about relating to people. Understanding how your clients and potential clients make decisions will help you relate to them more effectively. Linus Jarasius breaks down decision-making styles into three types:

1. Thinkers: They need all the facts, instructions and statistics. When they buy a camera, they want all the specifications down to the megapixels, and they'll want to read the instruction manual.
2. Feelers: These people make decisions on how they feel. They will make purchases based on the future experiences they can imagine with that purchase. Back to our camera example, when feelers buy a camera, they think about all the great memories they will capture.
3. Knowers: These are bulleted-pointed, fast-talking, bossy people. When they buy a camera, they look at the display, ask the cashier which one is the best value, and buy that one ten seconds later.

When you relate to people, you have to be a chameleon of sorts. My natural style is to be a knower. When I deal with a feeler, I have to slow down, listen better, and ask about the kids before I get down to business. Likewise, when I deal with a thinker, who tends to be extremely methodical and detailed, I have to talk slower and go over every detail, or they will think I am pushy and disrespectful.

Once you relate initially to your clients through their primary modality, they will make decisions from a secondary modality. For example, I am a knower first, but once I look at all the bullet points, I almost always end by making a decision with my feeler modality. Facts first, then emotions. Once you understand this simple process of relating to people, you will be able to do business with almost any personality!

Thinker, Feeler, or Knower?
Choose thinker, feeler or knower for the following statements:

I am a: _____

My spouse is a: _____

My largest referral account is a: _____

Pre-listing Package

Having a system before your appointment to educate your client about you and your selling systems is priceless. Make a professional first impression by dropping off a pre-listing package yourself. If you do not have the time, assign a team member to this task. This will demonstrate that you are systematized and prepared to handle the client's needs.

Include the following items in the pre-listing package:
- Your résumé and team page, listing their names and job responsibilities
- List of clients that are relevant to the future appointment, i.e. other properties sold in the neighborhood
- Past clients in a similar profession to the customer you are meeting (i.e. CEO's, athletes, physicians, school teachers, firefighters)
- Properties in a similar price range but a different neighborhood (i.e. lakefront, golf front)
- Samples of your marketing plan, such as a property flyer, brochures, postcards, print ads, and websites where the property will be posted
- Details of your company's success
- "All About You" form

By asking your client to complete an "All About You" form, you will gain valuable insight into the buyer's situation.

If you are sending a package to a local buyer, you can also include properties that match their criteria.

For relocation clients, we will add a questionnaire. This package also includes information on housing, arts and entertainment, education, and the local community.

Whether you have a seller, buyer, or relocation client, it is critical that you have an introductory system to make them feel important and that you are concerned about their specific needs. By providing your client with this information before your appointment, you not only save time that you would have spent going over basic information, but you also make an impression that is backed up by a system, truly creating a WOW experience.

The Ultimate Consultation

My philosophy has always been to spend quality time on the consultation finding out what the client wants, educating them on the process, and getting all the details you will need. If I completed everything at the consultation, then the rest of the process went smoothly and was less stressful. I know many professional coaches suggest a 20-minute consultation, but to me, spending plenty of time getting the details right initially not only builds trust, but also sets the pace for a great experience for my clients (and sets you up for referrals from them).

Getting off to a good start

Once the client has received the pre-listing package, we are ready for the face-to-face meeting. Sometimes we meet with people who know us or are referred to us, and other times we meet with people who do not know us at all. To reduce the anxiety of a salesperson showing up on the client's doorstep, I always use a tactic I learned during my first few years in the business. Once you enter the house, ask the client if you could set down your items, and then ask for a glass of water. Now you are no longer a "salesperson;" you are a guest in their house. You can watch their face relax into their role not as a client but a host.

Uncovering your client's motivation

Now that everyone is at ease, you are ready to begin the consultation. The purpose of my first question is to get the client to share with me their goals for buying or selling.

I ask them, "If you could organize this sale or purchase any way you like, what would that look like for you? For example, how long before the house sells? What is your ideal price?"

As you listen to their response, continue to ask why until you uncover their real motivation, that is, their emotional need for the transaction. Once you understand this part, you can weave it into your presentation and shape your responses to their objections accordingly.

Turn choices into options

As real estate agents, we know that there is a direct correlation between price and time, as well as between location, condition, and time. Help the customer understand the process by offering them options. For example, they could sell faster to move to meet their spouse who is relocating early, or remain behind longer to get the higher price they desire. By putting their choices into options, you guide them to the decision that will help them achieve their emotional need.

Triangle of Trust

If the customer was referred to you, the next step would be to review the Triangle of Trust, which we will delve into further in the next section. Reminding your customer about your mutual contact, the referral source, you will build trust faster and more easily get them committed to hiring you and following your advice concerning their property.

Present your information

After the client reveals their motivation and you have reminded them of the Triangle of Trust, it is time to find out if they have any questions regarding the pre-listing package. If not, then you can begin your listing presentation. I would recommend having this on a laptop or tablet for ease and professional appearance.

Create Your Consultation

Take a moment to create your consultation in the medium that best suits your business, i.e. laptop, tablet, hard cover book, etc.

- Why you?
  - Your information
  - Your team information
  - Company information
  - How you work
- Marketing
  - MLS
  - Website
  - Targeted lists
  - Other
- Process
  - Stage to list
  - Launch
  - Feedback
  - Contract to close overview
- Close for Business

Triangle of Trust

One of the most powerful ways to build trust quickly in the sales process is to use the Triangle of Trust.

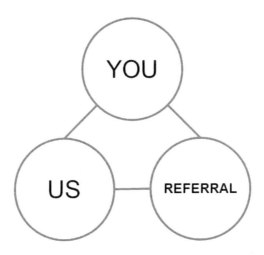

In this example, Julie, a past client, has referred Beth to me. I call her and set up our face-to-face appointment. Before starting my listing presentation, I ask Beth, "How do you know Julie?" After she tells me her story, I ask, "Do you trust Julie?" She responds, "Yes, I do!" Next, I tell her about my relationship with Julie and why I trust her, too.

I conclude with, "Beth, I want you to know that I have two relationships on the line. One is building trust between you and I, making sure I not only help you get your property sold, but that you also enjoy the process. I know when both of these events happen, you will feel comfortable referring your friends and family to me. Also, I have my long-time relationship with Beth. She has referred many clients to me, and I do not want to jeopardize that trust. Therefore, you should be comfortable knowing I will be working to continue these two very important relationships."

This puts the client at ease, knowing that you have taken a risk in completing their transaction.

Surveys

It is critical for you to survey every client to know how your customers feel about your service. This is a system to implement during both the listing and closing processes. The higher your scores, the more likely your clients will refer you to others who are in need of real estate assistance.

If you are in a market with an average of 60 or more days of selling time, send out a survey on day 45 to see how you are doing. At closing, ask your client to take a few minutes to have them fill out the form. Keep it convenient for them by e-mailing an editable format or mailing the form to them with a self-addressed envelope. This will change your business by alerting you to what adjustments you need to create a WOW experience.

Send a Survey
Send a survey to all your clients who are 45 days into the listing process or have closed within the last 60 days.

Here is an example of a survey form:

REALTY PARTNERS

DO YOU KNOW HOW TO HELP US?

We would like to "THANK YOU" for your trust in us to service your Real Estate needs. Now we need your help more than ever. We are always striving to be better at what we do, and hope you can help us to do that.

Even though our transaction is completed, our services do NOT stop there! We want to be your
YOUR REALTOR FOR LIFE!

Please take this time to tell us what you thought we did best and where you feel we could improve.

Why did you choose the Cooke Realty Partners? (circle)

Referred   Past Client   News Print   Financial Advisor

Lender   Web Site   Craig's List   Sign   Other

How well did we keep you informed throughout the transaction?

Excellent   Good   Fair   Average   Poor

Overall, describe the service you received from the Cooke Realty Partners.

Excellent   Good   Fair   Average   Poor

How would you rate your Cooke Realty Partners agent?

Excellent   Good   Fair   Average   Poor

Would you refer Cooke Realty Partners to someone you know?

Yes   No (why not) _____

What is one thing Cooke Realty Partners can do better?

_____

_____

Do you know anyone at this time that you could refer to us?

_____

_____
Client Signature

Rick Ruby: Five Tactics for WOW Service

Here are five tactics you can implement right now to WOW a client:

1. Return phone calls
- Real estate agents have a horrible habit of not returning phone calls. Return all phone calls within a two-hour time frame.

2. Have a voicemail system
- Your voicemail should have callback times and say when you are done for the day.
- For example, your voicemail should say, "Hi this is _____. I want to take great care of you today. I'll be returning calls up until 7 p.m. If you call me after 7 p.m., I will call you back first thing tomorrow morning."
- If you called my phone at 8 p.m. and got that message, you are either not going to leave a message, or you know I'm not going to call you back until tomorrow morning.

3. Keep refreshments in your car
- You must have a small cooler in your car and keep it stocked with bottled water, juice, protein bars, and candy bars every time you show property.
- After driving around for hours, your clients will appreciate having water and a snack.

4. Take the time to guide your client to a decision

- Most agents rush the process of showing houses, but if you show your clients a house that doesn't meet their needs, they aren't going to respect you as a real estate agent. Instead, spend 30 minutes before you go on the road helping them decide the four things they want. There might be 50 things they want. Get that down to two for him and two for her. Those are the four "mandatories" you've got to have.

- After you show property, sit in the driveway, pull out a piece of paper, and write down three things they liked and three things they didn't like about the house.

- Show the client no more than four properties at a time. Afterwards, go to a coffee shop, sit down and have a donut and a cup of coffee, and discuss the four houses you just looked at. What did they like? What didn't they like? Spend time consulting with them.

- Don't ask your clients if they want to buy that house. Instead, ask, "What would you pay for this house?" Everybody has a value that they see in something. We need to see if the client has a good sense of value. If the client thinks it's worth $200,000, but the listing price is $400,000, then there is a false sense of reality.

5. Follow Up

- Refer the client to the proper lender, and call them every Tuesday to update them on the process.
- Call them when they are approved and congratulate them.
- Bring non-alcoholic champagne to the closing to celebrate.
- Deliver a pizza and a liter of pop or a basket of cleaning supplies when they move.

WOW service is putting yourself in the client's eyes. Think about how you would want to be WOWed. Remember, WOWs are simple, not big. It's not like I'm giving away a Cadillac! I showed up and brought you pizza because you are moving today and I knew you would be stressed out… that is how you WOW a client.

MAXIMIZE YOUR TIME

Rick Ruby: Why Time Management Is Important

The most important thing I have ever learned in business is money management. The second is how to sell, the third is how to build a team, and the fourth most important thing I've ever learned in business is proper time management. Let me explain why time management is so important.

Busy but not productive

I have, right now, four mortgage offices, one major national mortgage company, one training company for real estate agents and lenders, and one mortgage recruiting company. So I really have seven businesses that all require my full attention, and they need me to act like I am full time in those jobs. If I didn't have proper time management, I wouldn't be able to give all of the people the proper time they wanted. So, I live on a tight schedule. From the minute I get in until the minute I go home, I am busy. I look at a lot of people that are busy, but they are not productive. The difference is, I'm highly productive because I'm aware of my time management.

Have a start time and end time

Too many real estate agents fly by the seat of their pants. Real estate agents wonder why they don't have consistency in their results, and it's because they don't have consistency in their efforts. You need a start time and a go home time every day. You have to start every day at the same time.

Managing time creates room to prospect

You need to spend four hours a day either talking to clients, meeting with listings, meeting with referral partners, or showing property. You have to prospect 20 hours a week. Look at your schedule every day and at the end of every day, mark down how many hours you prospected every day for 30 days. You are going to find you're not spending near enough time prospecting.

Print your schedule

Print your day-at-a-glance out of your calendar first thing and have it sitting on your desk every single day. It's not in your mobile device, and it's not in your computer. It is printed and with you at all times. You are much better off to have a printed schedule.

Delegate your schedule

The best way to have good time management is to have someone else be in charge of your schedule. If you have no assistant, your life is a mess. If you have one assistant, your life is half a mess. There are four jobs an agent's assistant has to do, so your life as a real estate agent doesn't get good until you have two or three assistants.

Time Blocking

Learning to use time effectively is the most challenging aspect of being a real estate agent. The term "independent contractor" creates an illusion that an agent can do what they want when they want. This illusion attracts many agents into the business. However, after a few years, when asked about their schedule, they will tell you that they work way too many hours. This is the result of that "what I want, when I want" mindset that causes agents to burn out and can also create issues with their family and marriage.

Can real estate agents really use a schedule?

To build a profitable business, you must have a time management system. I know you are thinking that real estate agents cannot live by a schedule. Our industry is too unpredictable, right? Wrong! I am here to tell you that after years of coaching by Rick Ruby and Todd Scrima, I am living proof that it does work. In fact, what I found is that when I work off a printed, time-blocked schedule, I actually have more freedom.

Freedom through structure

When we time-block our work week, we maximize our primary duties, which are prospecting, sales, and appointments. This frees us up to "work on" our business rather than "work in" our business. This means we get more accomplished in a day by working proactively on our priorities instead of working reactively on the urgent needs of the day.

When we do not have a daily plan, we get sucked into the "fires" and urgent issues that pull us off track. We allow the urgent matters to define our schedule and compete with the other important activities. The result of this behavior causes us to lose precious time and work late hours. After a while, this reactive approach takes a toll on our health and attitude and instead of accomplishing more, we find ourselves unable to be at our peak performance for our clients or our families.

Reeta Casey: The Ideal Work Week

Imagine a real estate agent who works 45 hours a week from 9 a.m. to 6 p.m., Monday through Friday, Saturday by appointment, and OFF on Sunday.

I know when you read that you chuckled and thought "no way!" And you are right — that is, if you expect to cut hours without changing your mindset and implementing The CORE Time Block System.

I can cite real estate agent after real estate agent who has been through our training and has made drastic changes to their schedule. Kendra Cooke in Nashville has a "date afternoon" with her son every Friday. Jim Bass from Maryland and Dayton Schrader, our senior coach from San Antonio, do not work weekends. It is possible to have that same freedom if you follow the process.

A Roadmap for Your Week
Let's review The CORE's ideal week, mapped out in our time-block system. The key components are as follows:

- **Personal time**
  - In order to achieve balance in your life, you will schedule time for YOU first. You work with your team and the public every day, and they count on you to be centered and strong. No one wants a martyr who works tons of extra hours, reacts immediately to every situation, and is pulled in a thousand directions. Instead, your clients and family want you rested, present, and engaging when you are with them. You can be that person

when you start your day with some personal time to recharge. Some examples might be to take the dog for a walk, meditate, read scripture, or listen to inspirational music.

- **Daily Team Meeting and e-mails**
  - If you do not have a team, then meet with yourself to know what you have for the day and get focused.

- **Power Hour**
  - We have established that in order for you to be profitable, you must prospect. SELLING is your main job, the most important daily activity, and really must be completed every day. The majority of your time each day should be spent in Green Time (the on-the-phone or face-to-face time with clients), which means either on the phone, face-to-face with clients, or talking to business people about how you can make money working together. Later in this chapter we will talk about "theme days," or prepared call lists so you do not have to struggle thinking about who to call each day.

- **Lunch**
  - Lunch is essential, not just to your health, but also to have time to share some food and beverage with a client, team member, or customer. I know some days require food on the run. Don't make that your daily routine; rather, make it your exception.

- **Appointments**
  ○ The afternoons are blocked for listing, buyer, and channel appointments. If you do not have all the time booked, then PROSPECT to fill those appointments. It will pay off!

  ○ When the phone rings and a customer calls for you to come list their house, DO NOT respond by saying, "When would you like me to come?" Doing this gives them total control of your schedule. (And you wonder why you work all the time?!) Instead say, "Thank you for the opportunity, and I can meet you Monday at 3 p.m., Tuesday at 6 p.m., or Saturday at 10 a.m."

  ○ This gives the client a sense of control and keeps you in charge of your calendar. Most importantly, you can keep that promise to loved ones to be home on time. Aren't you tired of calling your home only to say, "I am sorry, but I will be home late again"?

- **Follow Up**
  ○ The end of the day gives you time to follow up and go home. Note there is a designated time to go home. Be proactive and set two later evening appointment times for people who cannot meet you during the day. Also, select a weekend day to be by appointment only. What a life change when I started taking Sundays off and only went in on Saturdays when I needed to do so. This is how you bring a better quality of life to you and your family.

- **Family time**
  - We also designated family time. Your family is your number one client, so remember to include them on your schedule! You may need to rebuild some emotional credibility with the most important people in your life, so start now.

Take a look at the calendar on the following page to see how we recommend fitting all of these pieces into each day. Trust me when I tell you that if you implement this time-block system and set your mind to do it, then you will become a master of your time.

Ideal Work Week

THE CORE TRAINING INC.

	VIP-50 Favorite People Monday	Update Current Clients Tuesday	Database/ Hot Leads Wednesday	VIP-50 Favorite Past Clients Thursday	Business People/ Builders Friday	ALT Day
7-8am	Personal	Personal	Personal	Personal	Personal	
8am						
9am	Daily Meeting/Emails	Daily Meeting/Emails	Daily Meeting/Emails	Daily Meeting/Emails	Daily Meeting/Emails	
10am	Power Hour	Power Hour	Power Hour	Power Hour	Power Hour	Appointments
11am	Power Hour	Power Hour	Power Hour	Power Hour	Power Hour	Appointments
12pm	Lunch	Lunch	Lunch	Lunch	Lunch	Appointments
1pm	Appointments	Appointments	Appointments	Appointments	Appointments	Appointments
2pm	Appointments	Appointments	Appointments	Appointments	Appointments	Appointments
3pm	Appointments	Appointments	Appointments	Appointments	Appointments	Appointments
4pm	Appointments	Appointments	Appointments	Appointments	Appointments	Appointments
5pm	Follow Up	Appointments	Follow Up	Appointments	Follow Up	Follow Up
6pm	Go Home	Appointments	Go Home	Appointments	Go Home	Date Night
7pm	Family	Appointments	Family	Appointments	Family	Family

Delegating your schedule

The less you are in charge of your time, the more efficient you will become. Set up your schedule based on the ideal work week on the previous page and assign a team member to book your appointments in the designated time slots. Your goal is to arrive at work every day at the same time, get a copy of your printed schedule along with your call list, and follow it.

Having a team keeps you on schedule

I understand that this is a roadmap for your week and that there will be days when you must make adjustments. For example, if you have a relocation buyer in town for two days, you obviously have to spend time with them. This is where having a team will assist you. With a team, you would do the consultation, but have a buyer specialist (RP2) do the leg work. By keeping your focus on listings and having a team to manage your clients' needs, you will be more in charge of your time and better able to stay on task. This means more Green Time, and that translates to more referrals. In the next section, we'll talk more about building and leading your team.

Using your team to deepen client relationships

For me, having a team is the only way to enjoy the real estate industry while building deep client relationships. However, when I teach delegating the service of a listing or sales contract, I often hear agents say it is hard for them to hire a team member because their clients "only want them." This is a fear-based objection that that we can overcome when we explain to our clients that we provide the best service when the team executes the detailed paperwork, and touch point systems. There are so many details to each transaction, and I learned that I am not the best at every aspect of each deal!

How not to work evenings and weekends

We all know that one of our biggest challenges is living a balanced life, especially when we continue to work with buyers. Many times we have to work into the evenings, especially in the summer when daylight stretches, and when relocation clients fly in for a few intense days. This is why, as my business developed, I decided to focus on the listing side of my business and only took out buyers who were top clients or critical to the growth of my business long term.

When you have a great team to cater to your clients, you can focus on selling, listing appointments, corporate/channel meetings, and selling your team's services. As the selling agent, you spend time on the initial consultation, and then your team assists in the showing and servicing. Yes, you may get an offer on the weekend or evening, but the majority of the time, these negotiations can be done by phone. By having a buyer's agent who works evenings and weekends, you can still provide seven-day-a-week service. Be sure to give your buyer's agent one weekend off per month. Everyone on the team needs to stay healthy, focused, and balanced.

Setting your voicemail message

There are several small changes that can make a huge difference in managing your time. One is that I always let my clients know at the listing appointment that I am an early morning person, so my voicemail would state, "If this message is received after 6 p.m., it will be returned the next business day." I explained that they did not want me negotiating their biggest asset in the evening, since I am the sharpest during business hours. This system allowed me time to recharge in the evening with my family. I also did not set contract deadlines past 6 p.m. or on Sundays. The key is to explain what you do and why you do it to the client upfront so that you set the expectations for the relationship.

Printed Schedule and Theme Days

Now you have created a time-blocked schedule based on The CORE's ideal work week. Your RP1 sets up your schedule each day and books your appointments. The next and most critical step is to PRINT IT DAILY. While you may have a calendar and a version of your schedule on your computer and your phone, having it printed in front of you makes an enormous difference.

In addition to the printed schedule, your RP1 or assistant will also create and print call lists as described in the section on database. You will call a different list each day of the week. At The CORE, we call these our "theme days." No longer will you have to waste time starting your day thinking about who you should call, gathering their numbers, and getting ready to start prospecting. You know the night before what your goals are for the next day, and you are ready to rock and roll in the morning!

The CORE's **theme days** help you structure your prospecting:

- Monday: **Top 50 VIPs**
  - Favorite business people, builders, or vendors who can refer you business

- Tuesday: **Status Call Day**
  - Call your current listing clients and buyers in process with an update

- Wednesday: **Hot Leads and Database**
  - Hot leads are those who have not yet converted to a listing or a sale

- o Your database includes past clients, past client referrals, and personal friends
- o On the first week, call all those in your database whose last name starts with the letter A, followed by the B's, the next week for 26 weeks until you go through the entire alphabet. This is a simple system that results in you contacting your entire database two times per year.

- Thursday: **Top 50 Past Clients**
  - o Your favorite clients who refer you their friends, family, and coworkers

- Friday: **Cold calling new business people and builders**
  - o Aim to meet five new people per week to expand your brand awareness

Stop Being a "Pop Tart" Agent

Life balance begins with the structured schedule. In a business where so many people got in for the "freedom," what I have learned through Rick is only by being structured can you achieve that freedom. When he had me start working a schedule, I changed my mindset about being a "pop tart" real estate agent. This is the type of agent that pops up and runs out to an appointment, which many times turns out to be a waste of time. Having a time-blocked schedule to follow and a call list that follows the theme days will ensure that you are checking off all tasks that will help you meet your daily, weekly, monthly, and yearly goals. Make a commitment to work it and start NOW.

Create a schedule of your ideal work week

Using the example in this book, create your own ideal schedule. Include a start and a stop time every day, and remember to schedule time for your family and for yourself.

SUCCESS STORY: JIM BASS

A structured schedule gave me more – not less – freedom by allowing me to get more work done in less time.

Let me begin by stating, it's NOT natural for us as salespeople to be structured because our profession is such a reactive industry.

"Hey, Mrs. Real Estate Agent! Can I see this house right now? And by the way, I am standing right in front of it."

Or, "Hey, fellow agent! I have a contract on your listing, and by the way, there is a drop-dead provision or pre-settlement walk-through issues, and while everyone is sitting at the settlement table and the loan package has not arrived..."

The fundamentals of time management come down to "what we do, what we delegate, or what we discard." Once I began to focus on my highest dollar per hour activities: prospecting, building a team to cater to the clients, and managing my money, my income skyrocketed while my work hours declined.

I began by creating a "Perfect Work Week" calendar with my prospecting time blocked for 21 hours a week. Then I enlarged, framed, and mounted my oversized copy of a Perfect Work Week, highlighted with 21 hours of green time (direct money-making activities) and less red time (indirect money-making activities) on every team member's wall, including mine.

The only way I can consistently maintain prospecting more hours per week than less is by allowing my assistant to manage my distractions. Every morning on my desk, I am greeted with a copy of my daily call lists by theme day, MLS reports for expireds, team, and geographic farm activity; and a to-do list for today and tomorrow. This stack also includes a daily communication log, a "day at a glance," and a "week at a glance" so we can see what's coming at us.

Email management is essential to time blocking. Why? Because I can't be trusted... I am constantly looking for a gadget or deal to save me
time or make me more money. Then I'll see a listing I think I sold for sale with another agent, so I have to look it up in MLS only to discover I did not sell that one, but how did they get to that price…which leads me to tax records and pictures... and pictures. What's happened? I have lost 30, 60, 90 minutes… Please don't tell me I'm the only one! So I work e-mail from a vetted subfolder, not my inbox.

I make myself available for my assistant and my team three times a day: 8:30 a.m., 1 p.m., and 5 p.m. for email or issues review. This same structure worked when I was a team of one.

— **Jim Bass,**
Associate Broker/Co-Owner of Jim Bass Group/Real Estate Teams, LLC

SECTION THREE:
BUILD A TEAM
TO CATER TO YOUR
CLIENTS

RICK RUBY: TYPES OF LEADERSHIP

You are going to learn how to build a team, what your team members do, and how to delegate. You are going to get some great insight about team building in this chapter, but I think you have to learn that your leadership style is important. Great teams talk about leadership. So let's talk about the three types of leadership.

❖ **Lead By Example** – This is the best and most important type of leadership. Be on time. Be punctual. Be organized. Be fiscal. Be physically fit. Be well-groomed professionally. Lead your crew by example. That is the greatest way to lead your team. You're mentoring these people that come to work for you. You've got to show them good behavior, and show them how to act, so you've got to lead by example.

❖ **Servant Leadership** – This is based on the practice of Jesus, in that he loved people unconditionally. You have to love on your team. That means you have to feed them, hang out with them, look at their budgets, worry about their lives, give them good advice, and give them good direction. Servant leadership is when you are doing something special for people, such as birthday programs, parties, points of celebration, leaving early, etc. This is a great form of leadership.

❖ **Authority Leadership** – This means you are at a point with your team where you have built a mutual respect so that when you say something, it gets done. I'm not talking about being bossy, mean, or tough. I'm talking about you being an authority figure. You have a relationship with a person where you have done things for them, so when you say something, they don't take it personally or get offended. They just do it.

➤ Now, authority leadership is an earned behavior. What happens when someone comes in and starts bossing people around when they haven't earned the authority? That individual doesn't last very long, and people tend to have little or no respect for that person. So authority leadership is something that must be earned over time, kind of like how a parent earns authority leadership over time.

➤ However, a parent can lose that authority leadership when they are not in a relationship. There is a biblical formula that says discipline, without relationship, equals rebellion. That is something you have to remember with your team. If you are disciplining your team, and you don't have a relationship, they will rebel.

➤ I feel this is a good formula to look at for parenting or leading employees. I consider leading my employees like having 150 children, nephews, nieces, and cousins that I want to lead by example, that I've got to take care of, guide, and provide with a good environment.

BUILDING A GREAT TEAM

Why You Need a Team

At The CORE we believe you need a team of "A" players to keep you prospecting and bringing in business at your highest, most effective level. Having a team to cater to your clients is the key to building deep client relationships.

There are so many details to each transaction, and it takes a mindshift to understand that a salesperson is not the best qualified person to handle every aspect of the deal. Selling, negotiating contracts, and closing the deal are usually a salesperson's forté, but detailed paperwork and implementation of systems and structure are best executed by a detailed-oriented team member.

But my clients "only want me"

I hear real estate agents say it is hard for them to hire a team member because their clients "only want them." Oh, how we (and your clients) falsely believe only we can do the best job! Introduce your team to your clients early in the process and explain that they will get better service and faster responses by working with your team and not just you alone. Talking up your team's strengths in detail will give your clients confidence in your team members. And of course, you will truly win your clients over to the team model when your team provides WOW service through every step of the transaction.

The CORE Real Estate Team Model

The CORE real estate team separates job duties so that you have someone to set appointments for you, someone to manage your schedule and your transactions from contract to close, and someone else to focus on your buyers. This model frees you to focus on listings and prospect for more business. Our team model looks like this:

Team Leader: The Real Estate Agent
1. Team vision and leadership
2. Prospect to bring in 40 leads per month
3. Maintain 30 listings

Real Estate Partner 1 (RP1)
1. Manage the Team Leader's schedule
2. Manage the database, the Top 50 lists, and checklists
3. Manage buyer checklists and listings from contract to close

Real Estate Partner 2 (RP2)
1. Contact all buyer leads from listings, ads, and online and convert into two to four closed transactions per month
2. Show property and negotiate contracts
3. Work a set schedule and cover the Team Leader one day per week

Dialer
1. Talk to 20 people per day and dial 100 per week
2. Generate 10 leads per week
3. Train to be a Real Estate Partner 2

Your Team's Structure

Take a moment to write out your team's structure and list the top three priorities for each team member. See the examples below to assist you.

Real Estate Partner 1

TOP 3 DUTIES
1. Manage Team Leader's schedule
2. Manage database, Top 50 lists and birthday program
3. Manage listing and buyer checklists

1. Manage Team Leader's Schedule:
   - o Schedule all appointments
   - o Print daily schedule
   - o Confirm all appointment the day before
   - o Prepare a folder with all of the material needed for each appointment on daily schedule

2. Manage database, Top 50 and birthday program:
   - o Mail EOS/LOTH monthly
   - o Give team leader themed call list for power hour (i.e. database calls by letter of the wee, 12 of Top 50 Favorite People, etc)
   - o Schedule happy hours and client parties; implement birthday and gifts program systems

3. Manage Listing and buyer checklists
   - o Execute all listing plans
   - o Complete all 'contracts to close' steps

Real Estate Partner 2

TOP 3 DUTIES
1. Contact all buyer leads from listings, ads, and the Internet
2. Show property and negotiate contracts
3. Work a set schedule with a day off

1. Contact all buyer leads from listings, ads, and the Internet:
- o Take or return all buyer calls
- o Buyer consultation
- o Show property
- o Negotiate offers

2. Show property and negotiate contracts:
- o Use CORE showing checklist
- o Write and negotiate offers
- o Hold a minimum of two open houses per month

3. Work a set schedule with a day off:
- o Have a printed daily schedule with one day off per week
- o Attend daily team meetings
- o Attend one networking event per month

Dialer for Real Estate Agents

TOP 3 DUTIES
1. Talk to 20 people per day/100 per week
2. Generate 10 phone leads per week
3. Learn to be an RP2

1. Talk to 20 people per day/100 per week
   o Call database, current clients, referral partners
   o Call new referral partners for qualifying meeting
   o Constantly update and improve database and call lists
   o Follow theme days for calls

2. Generate 10 phone leads per week
   o Fill and update lead tracker
   o Schedule minimum of three appointments per week with prospects
   o Schedule minimum of two appointments per day with database, referral partners, and whales

3. Learn to be an RP2
   o Ask 10 questions per week to your Team Leader
   o Read one sales or real estate book per month
   o Take real estate licensing classes
   o Obtain a real estate license within six to twelve months

Rick Ruby:
Hiring and Training Employees

The first thing is job descriptions and job duties. You've got to sit down and write out what their job description is and what their job duties are. Later on, they will create their own job duties and descriptions, but early on, you've got to tell employees exactly what it looks like and give them a vision of what you are building. You've got to give them steps to follow.

You've also got to provide praise or correction after the work is done. "I like the work you did. It turned out really well!" or "I don't like the work you did. It didn't turn out very well." I will have my own employees work on projects around here, and sometimes I will not like it. So, I inform my employees that I don't care for it and ask them to come up with a better idea. It's not personal. When you are correcting employees, you've got to make sure you are correcting their behavior and not their personalities. That is a good leadership trait.

Basics of Delegation: The Daily Team Meeting

As the team leader, you are responsible for keeping the team running smoothly, and that means making sure all team members are on the same page. The daily team meeting is the tool to ensure everyone is focused and ready to roll on their priorities every day.

How to run a daily team meeting

Consistency is the key here, so start your meeting at the same time every day — we suggest 9 a.m. Follow the same format each day. Begin with a five-minute warm-up, then take about 15 minutes to review each person's top three priorities, and actual versus monthly leads, listing and sales goals. Follow the format below:

- **Warm-up** (about five minutes)
  - Find out how each person is doing
  - This allows time to build rapport at the start of the day rather than taking time around the coffee machine to chit chat
  - This is especially valuable on Monday mornings

- **Cover progress and goals**
  - What were your goals for the month?
  - How many active listings, sales, and leads?
  - Are you hitting your goals? If not, what actions will your team take?

- **Discuss the upcoming events for the week**
  - Make sure everyone can speak knowledgeably to your clients and business partners about your events

- **Ask each team member what their top two priorities are for the day**
  - This helps set your team up for success
  - This lowers the likelihood that your team will be distracted by fires that pop up throughout the day

- **Team Leader shares their schedule for the day**
  - You want your team to know your daily agenda
  - Designate a time when you will be available to answer questions

Use a form such as the one on the next page to keep your meeting organized and focused.

TEAM MEETINGS   Week of: _____

MONDAY (Top 50 FP)	TUESDAY (Status Calls)	WED (Hot Leads/Old Leads)	THURSDAY (Top 50 PC)	FRIDAY (Cold Calling)
Leads (70) ____ (mtd)	Leads (70) ____ (mtd)	Leads (70) ____ (mtd)	Leads (70) ____ (mtd)	Leads (70) ____ (mtd)
Listings (4) ____ (mtd)	Listings (4) ____ (mtd)	Listings (4) ____ (mtd)	Listings (4) ____ (mtd)	Listings (4) ____ (mtd)
Sales (7) ____ (mtd)	Sales (7) ____ (mtd)	Sales (7) ____ (mtd)	Sales (7) ____ (mtd)	Sales (7) ____ (mtd)
Hot Leads (20) ____	Hot Leads (20) ____	Hot Leads (20) ____	Hot Leads (20) ____	Hot Leads (20) ____
10 TOP 50	*UPDATES*	*DATABASE*	*HOT LEADS*	*BUSINESS BUILDERS*
Reeta ____	Reeta ____	Reeta ____	Reeta ____	Reeta ____
Julie (RP2) ____	Julie (RP2) ____	Julie (RP2) ____	Julie (RP2) ____	Julie (RP2) ____
Christina (RP2) ____	Christina (RP2) ____	Christina (RP2) ____	Christina (RP2) ____	Christina (RP2) ____
Alison (Listings) ____	Alison (Listings) ____	Alison (Listings) ____	Alison (Listings) ____	Alison (Listings) ____
Bruce (Mkt/Com) ____	Bruce (Mkt/Com) ____	Bruce (Mkt/Com) ____	Bruce (Mkt/Com) ____	Bruce (Mkt/Com) ____
Stephanie (Relo) ____	Stephanie (Relo) ____	Stephanie (Relo) ____	Stephanie (Relo) ____	Stephanie (Relo) ____
Monica (RP1) ____	Monica (RP1) ____	Monica (RP1) ____	Monica (RP1) ____	Monica (RP1) ____
Mark (Bus Dev) ____	Mark (Bus Dev) ____	Mark (Bus Dev) ____	Mark (Bus Dev) ____	Mark (Bus Dev) ____

The pipeline meeting
Wednesday's meeting will be longer than your daily meeting because in addition to the daily format, you will hold a pipeline meeting. Your pipeline meeting will last one to one and a half hours.

The first hour you will cover the agenda items above, along with your active listing clients and all contracts in the closing process. During the last 30 minutes, you will train your team in an area where you feel they need strengthening.

Why Have an Assistant?
It did not take me long to figure out that I needed help with all the details involved in a real estate transaction. I found myself prospecting, going on appointments, creating marketing, and working too many hours. I loved the interaction with the clients and negotiating the deals, but realized I had to hire someone to execute the promises I made to my clients. Therefore, I hired my first assistant my third year in the business.

I shared the time and expenses of my first assistant with another agent at my company. Even with splitting her time with another agent, I realized quickly that having her help me with the details created more time for me to be in front of clients and on appointments. This was the start of my team building and I never looked back.

Having a support person who schedules your time, confirms appointments, provides daily call sheets, and handles the details of your systems is a real game changer. This is where most agents get off task and waste precious time, preventing them from finishing important tasks and getting home at a reasonable time with their families.

When to Hire

When you reach two to three closings a month, it's time to hire a Real Estate Partner 1 (RP1). Remember, this is the position that executes all the administration work from the listing and buyer checklists to closing coordination, database and Top 50 List systems, and your personal schedule.

After you have an RP1 and your business increases from four to six closings per month, it is time to hire a Real Estate Partner 2 (RP2). The RP2 functions as a buyer's agent (compensated as an independent contractor) or showing agent (compensated as a W-2 employee). Remember, their primary responsibility is to show property and write contracts in order to create more time for you to prospect, build deeper relationships with your top clients, and build your listing inventory.

An analytical way to determine the value of hiring a team member is to calculate your working dollar per hour value. To calculate this number, take your taxable income from the previous year and divide by 12. Divide that number by 1,060 to get your dollar per hour rate.

Is the activity you are doing your highest and best value?

Moving Past the Fear of Hiring

Are you currently focused on selling and prospecting (activities that generate income), or are you doing tasks that can be done more efficiently by another person at a pay rate ranging from $10 to $20 per hour? The answer is clear.

I realize that it feels scary to hire an individual to work for you because you will be responsible for their paycheck. However, this is the step where you begin to become a real estate business person. Only by stepping out of your comfort zone, hiring a team member, and delegating administrative duties will you be able to prospect and build your business. Your business should not be solely dependent on you. After I pushed through my fear of hiring, I truly enjoyed having other people on my team to serve my clients at a higher level.

SUCCESS STORY: PHIL PUMA

The CORE showed me the value of building a team and the value of being a leader. I started with an assistant and a buyer's agent. As we continue to grow, we continue to hire more people.

Today, I have an operations manager, sales manager, executive assistant, listing coordinator, marketing coordinator, dialer, communication specialist, 10 buyer's agents, and two transaction coordinators. My business has grown more than 30% year over year, clients are happier, and I now have more clients and more time to prospect. My revenue has grown and my hours have decreased.

Hiring the team was not the difficult part; becoming an effective leader has been the challenge. Trust me, I work hard every day at being an effective leader.

One of the most important lessons that I have learned and continue to learn is that I need to lead my team, delegate to them, empower them, trust in them, and provide them structure, discipline, and love. I am no longer just a real estate agent; I am now running a business.

— **Phil Puma,**
President/Broker in Charge of Puma & Associates Realty, Inc.

MANAGEMENT AND LEADERSHIP

Rick Ruby: The Difference Between Management and Leadership

Management and leadership are two very big words with a very big difference.

- ❖ **Management** is excellence in execution.
  - ➤ Did you deliver a world-class experience every single time? Did you follow the ten steps? That's execution. Management is where you push motivation.

- ❖ **Leadership** is influence.
  - ➤ You are inspiring people to be more than they wanted to be. You're inspiring them to be different. You're helping them see a new vision for their life. Leadership is inspiration that you are drawn to.

To be a great leader, you must develop both of these skill sets.

The Keys to Management

In building a real estate business, we do not need a super large team to net the money we want to make; rather, we need to understand how to manage the team we have. As a CORE partner and president and founder of Summit Funding, Todd Scrima has learned a thing or two about being a great manager. Let's take a look at Todd's four keys to management and the biggest mistakes most managers make in each area.

1.

Centralized Scheduling
- One person is responsible for scheduling
- Daily evaluation if a client, loan or project is on schedule
- Everyone in the department easily knows if something is off schedule

2.

Specialized Jobs
- Every position has 3 main jobs, not 10 or 15
- The team is clear on exactly who does what
- Employees become "specialist" at what they do

3.

Formalized Management
- Someone is ultimately responsible for a department
- Regular reviews
- When a department is not running well, there is a process to discover and correct

4.

Standardized Work Flows
- Checklists
- Metrics and timelines for every process and procedure
- The entire organization does it the same

The Biggest Mistakes Managers Make

- **Inconsistent scheduling**
  - The average team leader fights holding meetings and events with the energy they could use instead to become great! I don't think an NFL team gets to cancel practice because they don't want to go.
- **Confusion on job duties**
  - It is the curse of a small business. Most employees have entirely too many jobs and they do not know which duty to focus on and prioritize. Don't be afraid to grow your team. You will be amazed at how much easier it is to have a five-person team than a two-person team. A larger team allows you to have specialized job duties.
- **Formalized management**
  - Every team needs a point person to hold others accountable for their responsibilities. Without regular reviews, team members do not have have a way of growing in their position, and you do not have a way of improving your business.
- **Standardized work flow**
  - Requiring team members to follow checklists and timelines to provide services the same way every single time is the biggest inconsistency in most businesses. This inconsistency prevents small businesses from being able to scale. If you don't learn to provide consistent structures for every step of every transaction, your business will never be able to blow up.

Leadership 101

Most simply defined: Leadership is influence.

We influence clients and potential clients every day in the sales process. Now that you have a team, it is time to understand your team members as well as your clients. Learning how to provide sound leadership will take the fear out of building a team.

In John Maxwell's *Five Levels of Leadership* (Center Street, 2013), we learn about how we grow as a leader. Take a look at the chart and see where you fall as a leader. How can you grow to the next level?

5 Levels of Leadership

"Long Term – Your Leadership Will Determine Your Long Term Success!"

Level 1: Respect — • People follow you because of who you are and what you represent

Level 2: Reproduction — • People follow you based on what you have done for them

Level 3: Results — • People follow you because of what you have done

Level 4: Relationships — • People follow you because they like you

Level 5: Position — • People follow you because they must

Common Mistakes People Make in Developing as a Leader

- **Reproduction**
  - Listen to the subtle comments that team members make when they are seeking help
  - Example: A negative response to a simple "hello"

- **Not living by the Golden Rule**
  - Treat all your team members with respect
  - Remember, each position is essential to creating a WOW experience

- **Lack of transparency**
  - Express your emotions with graciousness (no swearing or yelling)
  - Do not shy away from confrontation, just address it

- **Emotionally driven**
  - Do not react and get so emotionally biased
  - Be direct and keep your cool

Train Yourself to Be a Leader

At the back of this book, you will find a recommended reading list that will help you develop your sales, management, and leadership skills. We also recommend seeking out leadership training. All CORE partners and coaches have attended numerous classes at Rapport Leadership, and we have found that it has increased our leadership skills.

Class is in Session!
Contact **Rapport Leadership International** *to register for their classes.*

www.rapportleadership.com
(702) 697-5334
5735 S Sandhill Road,
Las Vegas, NV 89120

SECTION FOUR:
COUNT THE
MONEY

HOW TO TRACK YOUR MONEY

Rick Ruby: Why Prepare a Profit & Loss?

Well, let me tell you something. The most important thing I've learned in business is money management. You have to learn how to manage your money. Every single business has to run a Profit & Loss statement. Take a lemonade stand for example. Your parents give you the lemonade and cups. You sell lemonade and keep all of the profits. Is that a business? No. That's your mommy and daddy giving you money to sell lemonade.

That's how many real estate agents run their business. To run your business properly, you've got to look at all of the revenue and subtract all of the expenses. What is left over is profit, and then you need to set 30% aside for taxes. After that, whatever is left is your net income.

All of my companies, from the smallest of five employees to the biggest company of 1,200 employees, run the same P&L system. It is printed every month and we look at it every month. Every publicly traded company prepares a Profit & Loss statement. If you don't prepare a Profit & Loss, you are a lemonade stand for your mom and pop. You will never survive or accumulate any wealth. You will never do anything special with your finances or your business.

I don't want you to be the agent who flies by the seat of his pants, does a little business, and in 15 years is doing the exact same business. I guarantee, if you follow me, every year you will grow 20%. You will hire more staff, save more money, pay more taxes, and accumulate wealth. That is what will happen when we prepare a Profit & Loss.

The Basics of the Profit & Loss

The most important form a real estate agent must know and understand is the Profit & Loss to ensure that the service they are providing is yielding a profit.

Too often real estate agents think the check cut from the brokerage goes directly into their personal account. WRONG! You have to pay to run your business, and you must pay Uncle Sam out of every check, or you will get behind. There is nothing more depressing than discovering on April 15th when taxes are due that you do not have the money available in your savings account because you used it during the year. STOP! You are not a W-2 employee, so you cannot think about your money like one.

The commission you generate is the result of your sales service. That check belongs to the brokerage and is returned with the HUD Statement in order to deduct any referral fees or splits. After those deductions, the remaining amount goes to you or your business entity.

Here is the important part: *That check does not go home with you.* Instead, deposit it into a business checking account from which at the end of every month you will pay all your bills and set aside estimated taxes. After all that, THEN what is left over goes to you personally.

How to complete a P&L

Now I want to review the Profit & Loss form so you know how the money flows. You can follow along with the blank P&L. Understanding this form will help you start thinking like a business owner, resulting in better informed money decisions.

Section 1: Expenses

The left side of the form is for expenses.

Office expenses are recurring monthly expenses such as rent, office phone, printing, and contractual commitments such as Zillow and Trulia. Listing out these regular monthly expenses will keep you from making too many long-term commitments.

Wage expenses is where you list the monthly salary for any team members as well as your own salary, if you take one.

Miscellaneous expenses include items such as dues, signs, new equipment, happy hour expenses, and random gifting.

Personal expenses refers to those items that you pay for with your business checking account, for example, a lease on your car, your personal cell phone, or your health insurance.

The total of these four types of expenses will show you the cost of running your business each month.

Sections 2 and 3: Income

The right side of the form lists your income.

Section 2 lists outside revenue such as referral fees, processing fees, and your portion of the buyer's agent fees.

Section 3 lists your income from the direct sell of houses. This section deals with the agent's direct income, which keeps pure the total and average revenue per house sold.

Section 4: Putting it all together

In Section 4, you combine your total income from outside revenue (Section 2) and personal revenue (Section 3). From that total, you subtract your monthly expenses (total from Section 1). Finally, you deduct 25% in estimated taxes to set aside in a savings account until your taxes are due. The remaining balance is your after tax income that you will bring home to your personal account.

PROFIT AND LOSS

Month: January   Year:

SECTION 1	Expenses
OFFICE EXPENSES	

SECTION 2	Income
OUTSIDE REVENUE	
TITLE CO. REVENUE	
REFERRAL FEES	
PROCESSING FEES	
BUYER AGENTS/LOAN REPS	
Name & # of units:	

Subtotal	$0.00
WAGE EXPENSES	

COMPANY INCOME	
TOTAL OTHER REVENUE	$0.00

SECTION 3	PERSONAL REVENUE
PERSONAL REVENUE FROM	
PAY LOG	

Subtotal	$0.00
MISCELLANEOUS EXPENSES	

# OF UNITS	
REVENUE PER UNIT	
divide revenue by # of units	#DIV/0!
TOTAL REVENUE	$0.00

Subtotal	$0.00
PERSONAL EXPENSES	

SECTION 4	NET INCOME
Section 2 TOTAL	$0.00
Section 3 TOTAL	$0.00
TOTAL GROSS INCOME	$0.00
Subtract Section 1 Expenses	$0.00
TAXABLE INCOME	$0.00

Subtotal	$0.00
Total Expenses:	$0.00

x 25% for Uncle Sam (x.25)	$0.00
After Tax Income	$0.00

Taxable Income

COMPANY FLOAT BALANCE:	SALARY:	TAXABLE INCOME: $0.00 (from Section 4)
TAX BALANCE:		

COMPANY DEBT TOTAL:	PROFIT: $0.00 (Section 2-1)	PERSONAL EXPENSES RUN THROUGH COMPANY: $0.00
PROJECTED YEAR END GROSS TAXABLE PAID TO OWNER: $0.00 (Gross tax YTD divided by # of months x 12)		GROSS TAXABLE PAID TO OWNER YTD: $0.00 (TAXABLE INCOME + SALARY from all P&L's YTD)

REETA CASEY AND RICK RUBY

The Numbers to Net $300,000+

What is my goal? This is the critical first question when building your business. Knowing your numbers helps you approach this answer analytically rather than emotionally. When you understand the Profit & Loss form, you can use it to create your real estate business model by working backwards from where you want to be.

Let's use $300,000 in annual net taxable income as an example target. We'll use taxable income, since tax brackets vary among us.

Example P&L for $300,000 annual net taxable income

I will explain the steps, and you can follow along on the numbered example P&L. Once you understand how to do this, you can use this exercise to create your perfect model.

Section 4

1. <u>Taxable Income</u>: Under the words "taxable income," we'll write our annual target. In this example, that is $300,000. In the column, we'll put the monthly net, which is $25,000 ($300,000 divided by 12).

2. <u>Section 1 Expenses</u>: Your expenses should be 50% of your revenue. Therefore, beneath the words "Section 1 Expenses," write $150,000 and in the column, put $12,500 ($150,000 divided by 12).

3. Total Gross Income:
   a. Add $150,000 in annual expenses to our annual income goal of $300,000.
   b. Write $450,000 under "total gross income goal" and $37,500 in the column ($450,000 divided by 12).
   c. Remember that this number is the combination of your personal production and any outside revenue.

Section 3

4. Personal Revenue: In this example, the agent sold three houses (# of units). Let's say the average was sales price $500,000. After the company split, the agent receives a check of $12,000 for each transaction. The total for three sales is $36,000.

Section 2

5. Total Other Revenue: The example shows a referral check, four process fees at $50 each and two BPO's for $150 each. This gave the agent a total of $1,500 in other revenue.

Section 1

6. Expenses: Remember that this section lists regular office expenses ($5,730), wage expenses ($4,545), miscellaneous expenses ($1,275), and personal expenses run through the business ($950).
7. Total Expenses for Section 1:
   a. The total monthly expenses are $12,500, which is 50% of our example monthly income goal.

    b. You MUST remember that if you are not on track to close your $37,500 in income, you must cut back or not get paid at the end of the month.

    c. A profitable business must yield a profit at the end of a thirty day period. In this example, the business must net $25,000 for the agent to hit their goal.

The Bottom of the P&L: Business Snapshot

8. <u>Company Float Balance</u>:

    a. This is a savings account with one month of Section 1 expenses, in this case $12,500.

    b. This amount should be kept in there at all times in case of an emergency so you do not have to dip into your personal account.

9. <u>Tax Balance</u>:

    a. You need to deduct your "estimated taxes" prior to writing yourself a check to take home. This money is not yours, so it is easier to never claim it or cash it.

    b. By writing a check for this amount and depositing it into your business savings, you will have the money to pay your estimated taxes at moment's notice.

    c. Most agents generate a sale in the next tax year to pay the previous taxes, so they never get ahead! You WILL NOT accumulate wealth by following that plan.

10. <u>Salary</u>: If you take a salary, write the amount on this line, but make sure it is a number you can hit every month.

11. <u>Taxable Income</u>: Take this number from the line in Section 4, which is the total revenue after subtracting expenses.

12. Company Debt Total: If you have borrowed money to put into the business or have recurring business credit card debt, write that amount here.

13. Profit:
    a. Take the Section 2 total minus Section 1 total.
    b. For many agents, this number is initially in the negative. Just think, if the money coming from sources covered your expenses, then everything you close is 100% profit to YOU!

14. Personal Expenses Run Through Company: Simply write the subtotal from that category in Section 1 ($950.00).

15. Gross Taxable Paid to Owner YTD: Take the "taxable income" number from Section 4 ($25,000) and add it to the number on the year's previous P&L's. This example P&L is for January, so $25,000 is the total YTD.

16. Projected Year End Gross Taxable Paid to Owner:
    a. Take the "gross taxable paid to owner YTD" number ($25,000) and divide by the number of months. Since this is a January P&L, divide by 1.
    b. Multiply by 12 (average monthly income multiplied by 12 months in a year).
    c. The result is the income number you are on track to make.
    d. If this number does not meet your goal ($300,000 in this example), then you must sell more or reduce your expenses.

REETA CASEY AND RICK RUBY

PROFIT AND LOSS

Month: January		Year: 2015			
SECTION 1		**Expenses**		6	
OFFICE EXPENSES					
1 Rent	$	1,000.00	**Section 2**		**Income**
2 Postage	$	300.00	OUTSIDE REVENUE	$	
3 Printings	$	500.00	TITLE CO. REVENUE		
4 Supplies	$	150.00	REFERRAL FEES		$1,000.00
5 Marketing	$	1,500.00	PROCESSING FEES (4)		$200.00
6 Training/Coaching	$	400.00	BUYER AGENTS/LOAN REPS		
7 Website	$	300.00	Name & # of units		
8 Copy	$	400.00	BPO's		$300.00
9 Photography	$	900.00			
10 Top Producer (CRM)	$	80.00			
11 Paper	$	200.00			
12					
Subtotal:		$5,730.00			
Wage Expenses					
13 RP1 $36,000		$3,000.00			
14 Closing Coordinator		$795.00	COMPANY INCOME		
15 ($300 per file)			TOTAL OTHER REVENUE	$1,500.00	5
16 Taxes		$750.00			
17			Average Sales Price $500,000 @ 3%x80%		
18			**SECTION 3**	**PERSONAL REVENUE**	
19			PERSONAL REVENUE		
Subtotal:		$4,545.00	FROM PAY LOG	$36,000.00	4
Misc. Expenses					
20 Happy Hour		$175.00	# OF UNITS	3	
21 Signs		$100.00			
22 Lock Box		$50.00	REVENUE PER UNIT	$12,000.00	
23 Dues		$200.00	divide revenue by # of units	$4,000.00	
24 Meals		$600.00			
25 Gifts : $50 per person		$150.00	TOTAL REVENUE	$36,000.00	
26					
Subtotal:		$1,275.00			
Personal Expenses			**SECTION 4**	**NET INCOME**	
27 Auto		$600.00	Section 2 TOTAL	$1,500.00	
28 Phone		$150.00	Section 3 TOTAL	$36,000.00	
29 Gas		$200.00	TOTAL GROSS INCOME		
30			$450,000	$37,500.00	3
31			Subtract Section 1 Expenses		
Subtotal:		$950.00	$150,000.00	$12,500.00	2
			TAXABLE INCOME		
Total Expenses		$12,500.00	$300,000.00	$25,000.00	1
		2	x 25% for Uncle Sam	(x.25)	
			After Tax Income	$	

Taxable Income

8	COMPANY FLOAT BALANCE ___$12,500*___	10 SALARY _____	11 Taxable Income ___$25,000___
9	TAX BALANCE _____	14	
12	COMPANY DEBT TOTAL ___$0.00___	13 PROFIT ___<11.00>___ (Section 2-1)	Personal Expenses run Through Company ___$950___
16	PROJECTED YEAR END GROSS TAXABLE $300,000** PAID TO OWNER _____ (Gross Tax YTD divided by # of months x 12)	GROSS TAXABLE PAID TO OWNER YTD ___$25,000___ (TAXABLE INCOME + SALARY from all P&L's YTD)	15

*One month of Section 1 Income   **$25,000/1(January)x12

128

Now you can get a true understanding of what your business should produce and how to manage it in order to hit your goal. How empowering it is to know your numbers! So prepare your Profit & Loss statement NOW and start creating the money goal you want to achieve.

Profit & Loss

Take a moment to fill out your own Profit & Loss statement and learn your company's numbers.

Personal Money

This is the most emotionally charged subject in our lives. Money is necessary to provide for our families and to help others. However, many real estate agents are afraid to take an honest look at their personal income and expenses. Hiding behind ignorance impedes us on our path to success. To become true business people, we must learn to manage our money in our personal lives.

The Personal Family Budget

At The CORE, we hold each other accountable to not only our income goals, but our savings goals. Making a lot of money is only half the battle to achieving wealth. When we track and save our personal money, we are well on the way to achieving financial freedom.

We do this by using a form called the Personal Family Budget. Complete the budget on the first day of every month, using all paychecks and bills that you received the previous month. This way, you only touch your money once per month. We will go into further detail later in the chapter.

Let's take a closer look at the form itself. You will find an example on the following pages.

Column 1:
- List all your expenses for that month.
- If you carry a debt balance, write that number in parenthesis beside that expense.
- For example: Visa ($5,342)

Column 2:
- Write the minimum amount you must pay each month.
- For your utility bills, etc., write the exact amount that appears on your bill.
- If you have an irregular expense, i.e. a vacation or birthday, do not list it in column 2.
- Total your column 2 expenses. This is your *survival number* — how much money it costs to maintain your current lifestyle.

Column 3:
- This column tracks what you did with all of your monthly income
- List the total amount you paid for each expense that appears in column 1.
- After paying bills, you will put money into savings. That amount appears in column 3.
- The total for column 3 must match the total for column 5

Column 4:
- This is a tally of your savings, which includes paying down debt.
- If you paid extra on revolving debt, put the difference in this column.
- For example, if you owed $2,000 on your house, but you paid $2,500, you will write $500 in column 4.
- Write the amount you put into savings in both column 3 and column 4.
- Total column 4. This is your total savings for the month.

Column 5
- List all paychecks that your household received the previous month.

The Bottom of the Form

Money Market Balance: How much do you actually have in your money market or savings?

Money Market Float: This is a target number. You want to maintain three times your survival number in your savings at all times.

Column 4 divided by Column 5: This gives you a percentage saved. Your goal is 20% each month.

$ Saved YTD: Add your column 4 total from each month of the year.

Cash Net Worth: This is the total of your money market account, 401K/IRA balance, mutual funds, and stocks.

Total Net Worth: This is your cash net worth plus any equity you have.

Giving YTD: We strive to live in gratitude, graciousness, and generosity. Part of that comes in giving back from our abundance.

PERSONAL FAMILY BUDGET

MONTH: _____ YEAR: _____

1	2	3	4	5
NAME OF BILLS	MO OWED MIN	MO/TOTAL PAID	AMOUNT SAVED	TOTAL PAYCHECKS
HOUSE				
AUTO				
STUDENT LOANS				
CREDIT CARDS				
B/S				
B/S				RENTS
				DIVIDENDS
				REFUNDS
ELECTRIC				
GAS				
PHONE				
CABLE				
SEWER				
WATER				
DRY CLEANING				
YARD MAINT				
DAY CARE				
CELL PHONE				
INSURANCE				
TRASH PICKUP				
INTERNET				
NEWSPAPER				
GAS				
GROCERIES				
DOCTOR				
GIVING				
SPENDING $$$				
MISCELLANEOUS				
IRA- SEP				
MONEY MARKET				
401K				
Totals				
Totals				
	SURVIVAL NUMBER	TOTAL CHECKS WROTE	TOTAL MONTHLY SAVED	NET INCOME FOR MONTH

Money Market Balance _____

Money Market Float _____
needs to be 1 % survival #)

Column 4 div. column 5 equals
% saved this month _____

$ Saved YTD _____

Cash Net Worth _____

Total Net Worth _____

Giving YTD _____

Net Worth

401k Balance _____

Mutual Fund Balance _____

Stock Balance _____

Equity in Home _____

Equity in Rentals _____

133

Rick Ruby:
The Six Steps to Financial Freedom

I want to share a story with you about how I started.

I was a loan rep and I owned a little mortgage brokerage. I was in my twenties and doing really well, making a lot of money and having fun. I had a Buick Riviera, a cell phone in a bag with the antenna that goes on top, a nice house, two new cars, a hot rod in the garage, nice clothes, and good vacations. I was really enjoying life.

There was a guy in my office building named Bill. Bill was about 55 years old at the time, and he wore a suit every day, but it wasn't really that sharp. His clothes didn't fit well, and they weren't that fashionable. He had a beard and he wasn't very groomed, and his hair was kind of unruly, but Bill and I became friends.

I walked into his office one day and he was literally gluing the sole back onto his shoe, and I picked on him about it. Another day, the hem came undone from his cuffed pants, and he stapled the hem. Also, this guy worked out of whatever office in the building that was vacant. He would run the phone line from the closet, drop the wires, and work out of an empty suite. He really was like a homeless guy in the office. But I liked him! He was my friend.

So, one day I was picking on Bill, and he said, "Rick, I've had it with you. How much money do you have?"

I said, "Bill, I made $112,000 last year."

He said, "I didn't ask how much money you made. I asked how much you have in the bank."

I said, "Bill, I honestly don't know. My wife pays all the bills. She handles everything."

He took out a piece of paper and drew a line down the middle. "I want you to go home tonight and write assets on the right and debt on the left."

I went home that night with my wife, Nancy, and we wrote it all down. I went in the next morning, and I was proud. I had $68,000 in assets and $72,000 in debt, not counting two car loans, a hot rod line of credit, a mortgage and a second mortgage. So, I go in to see Bill and I'm all proud and puffed up. And he says, "Why are you so happy?

I said, "What are you talking about? I'm in pretty good shape. I'm almost even."

He said, "That's horrible. You've got $72,000 in unsecured debt with a 17% interest rate. You're in horrible financial shape."

I said, "Bill, you don't know what you're talking about."

He pulled out a piece of paper. It was a statement from one of his financial planners, and it showed $6.3 million in the bank. All of a sudden, I'm in awe of Bill. Bill's got all this money, and here he acts like he's broke, and I act like I'm rich. So I learned a valuable lesson right there that it doesn't matter what you appear to be, it matters what you actually have.

So, Bill taught me about money. He said, "Rick, I can quit working right now. With 5% interest in bonds, I can get $300,000 a year and do whatever I want, but you're broke and you have to scramble every day of your life."

Now I've surpassed my mentor in money in the bank. I have one mortgage left, and it will be paid off in a year and a half. I'm definitely not working for survival, not for stuff, not for financial security. The only reason I'm doing this now is to change the planet, my legacy in the industry, and I want to have fun. The reason I tell you how much money I have is so that you know I'm credible.

Let me tell you my six steps to financial freedom:

1. Track every dollar in and every dollar out.
- Have one bank and three accounts: a checking account to pay your bills, a savings account for your spending money for purchases under $20, and a money market account for your float (three times your survival number).
- Pay your bills once a month. It's easier to allocate to savings and debt reduction when you're paying once a month. Pay your utilities and allow yourself money for groceries, gas, and insurance.

2. Pay off all revolving debt first.

- Carry two credit cards: one business, one personal.
- If you currently have credit card balances, set those aside and get new accounts with zero balances. Don't use the old ones anymore. Instead, you're going to pay down your debt. This is going to be a two-year process. You didn't accumulate debt overnight, so you're not going to pay it off overnight.
- The key to my program is to pay off your credit card every month. No matter what you put on it, you have to pay it off. It's cheaper to pay $50 in therapy to deal with your guilt than to go guilt shopping.
- While you're paying down debt, put two-thirds of your money toward debt and one-third toward your float. You need to build up your float because if something comes up, you don't want to go into more debt.

3. Accumulate a float account.

- A float account is three times your survival number. I need $36,000 in my money market to be safe. That's three months of bills paid in a reserve account.
- We pay things off out of cash flow and income. We do not buy things out of assets. Assets are for one thing: to grow. Finance purchases and pay them off out of cash flow.

4. Invest in a retirement account
- Before investing in anything else, you want to max out your 401K and IRA. Up until you have $250,000 in investments, only buy mutual funds.

5. Invest in the stock market
- First, invest in index funds, then managed money.
- The last way is individual stocks. Never own more than five to eight stocks, and buy really good companies. I've been buying Disney for 20 years, Nike for five years. These are companies I really, really like, and they're big and strong. There's not a lot of risk with these companies.

6. Pre-pay your mortgage
- Why would you pre-pay on your mortgage? It's an investment. My house payment is at 3.5 percent, so when I pre-pay, it comes off the back of the loan, so it's like a 3.5 percent net gain. It's a nice, small investment.

I've gone from $72,000 in credit card debt 31 years ago, to $8.3 million in the stock market. It's a long journey. I'm a high school dropout. If I can do this, you can do this. The key is, you have to surrender to people who are where you want to go. You're not going to figure it out on your own.

This is not complicated; this is a system. Just follow the rules. Remember, I'm teaching you systems to be the best you can be so you can go out and enjoy your life.

Reeta's Personal Budget Success Story

I want to thank Rick for his regular commitment to review my personal budget for more than 15 years. When I began, I hated to take time out every month only to get depressed when I looked at my numbers. It seemed like such a huge mountain to climb from no savings to building financial freedom.

There were many times during the process when Rick would yell at me for not saving. Finally, I became aware of my spending habits and addicted to saving money. WOW! What a charge from seeing that number go up versus the impulsive shopping trips I took when I felt like I "deserved" to buy something because of all the hours I was working.

By changing my mindset, my husband, Pat, and I were able to build our dream home on the lake and have a comfortable life. For our thirtieth anniversary, we took a 24-day trip around the world with National Geographic! I never thought I would have the money or the time to spare for such a dream, but we did.

Now after 15 years, I am ready and financially able to cut back my schedule and just direct my focus on The CORE part time. It's funny how we get into our routines year after year, and then we look up to see that we have hit our financial goals. This would not have been possible without the Six Steps to Financial Freedom that Rick taught me and the thousands of other people who will also tell you how it changed their lives.

My next goal is to work with Pat to pay off our mortgage. Then we can truly spend our time as we choose and enjoy the years in pursuing our passions and in our charity work. I am grateful for what Rick has shared with me, for holding me accountable, and for caring. Changing our mindset is not easy, but with The CORE coaching, I did it, like many others who are doing it, too.

Life is too short not to make it count, so bring it on! The change is worth it.

LIFE BALANCE

Rick Ruby: The Importance of Life Balance

You have choices for how you live your life.

I worked 80 hours a week, I got divorced, my kids didn't want to hang out with me. That's one option. Or you work 40 hours a week, you fall in love, you go on a date every week, you exercise, you hang out with your kids, you visit your mom and dad, you hang out with your cousins, you have a bunch of friends, you pursue your purpose in life which is more than making money.

Those are your options:
- **Option A**: You work 80 hours a week and end up divorced, fat, and unhappy.
- **Option B**: You work on balance, you have it all, and your life is joyous.

So which do you choose, misery or joy? Choose right now.

I pick joy! Joy means I have to work out twice a week. I have to go to church on Sunday. I have to read my Bible every day. I have to go on a date with my wife. I have to run my business on a structured 40 hours a week. I have to save money for my retirement. I had to fund my kids' college funds. I have to see my friends by golfing and playing poker once a week. I have to talk to my mom, sisters, nieces and nephews.

Just by talking about it balance is *overwhelming*. To have it all is very difficult and because it is, most people don't. I know so many rich people that are miserable because they don't have balance. Their work is their life.

I work to have a life. My life is not my work. That should be your theme of the day.

I'm going to give you two quotes that I love:

"I did my best and my best is good enough."
- I think it is very important that you go to work, give your best, and then you let it go.

"Nothing comes to those that wait."
- You've got to pursue life with vigor and go after it with all you have.

I've been both guys: overweight, miserable, and divorced; and in love, rich, happy, and fit. The second guy is much more fun! That guy requires that I spend so much time working on my balance.

My schedule is full from 9 a.m. to 7 p.m. Every week I go on a date with my wife, Britt. I talk to both of my grown-up children once a week at a scheduled time. I have a Bible study every Wednesday night from 5:30 p.m. to 6:30 p.m. I'm in the gym Wednesday night from 8-9 p.m. and Friday from 4-5 p.m. I work out with a trainer because I want to get the most done. I have business and life coaches. I'm involved in charities. I give 10% of my money away. I go golfing with my friends every Sunday afternoon after church or we have a bonfire and watch football. I talk to my mom every two weeks. I visit with my nieces and nephews. We just

142

had a family reunion at my mountain log cabin. We had a great time with 35 relatives. I have been working on my life balance for 15 years. I do the Wheel of Life two or three times at the end of every year. (This is an activity you will be doing in this chapter.)

Now, all of these things sound great, but I'm telling you, it has required so much work to get balance in my life. It is so hard to have it all, and that is why most people don't have it all. In the end, they are frustrated, depressed, and annoyed. I see so many athletes, movie stars, and politicians who are depressed, frustrated, self-medicated with drugs and alcohol, and addicted to shopping and gambling.

I think true balance comes from love. I think it comes from a relationship with God. I think that is the place to start. You've got to have a foundation to build on. I believe that is what it takes to have true balance in life.

The Wheel of Life

One thing we really love about The CORE Training is our holistic approach to your business and life. We teach you systems and structure to build a profitable business so you can pay off debt, save money, and build wealth. As a result, you will enjoy a higher quality of life and be able to strike a healthy balance of time spent with friends, family, and work.

At our Summit events twice each year, we do an exercise that helps you take a hard, honest look at seven areas of your life. You'll find example forms on the next two pages. To see how your Wheel of Life currently looks, follow the instructions below:

1. Rate each area on a scale from 1 to 10.
    a. One is the worst, maybe even non-existent.
    b. If you are perfectly balanced in the area, then it would be a 10.
2. Once you have ranked each area, plot the results on the chart.
    a. You'll count out from the center of the wheel.
    b. For example, if you ranked your love life a three, count three dots out from the center of the wheel.
    c. If you ranked yourself at a 10, make a mark closest to the tip of the arrow.
3. Connect the dots and see how round your wheel is.

This will show you what areas of your life are most out of balance, and The CORE can teach you how to create the balance that you desire. The last step is to complete the form "Where Will You Be" and decide how you will improve your life in the next year by setting goals in each of the seven areas.

Wheel of Life

Fill out the Where Are You Now? form and plot the data on the Wheel of Life form to find out just how balanced or unbalanced your life is. Use Where Are You Now to set personal and professional goals for the upcoming year.

Where are you now?
What is your biggest struggle in each area?

	7 Boxes of Life	Rate 1-10
Work	1.) 2.)	
Money	1.) 2.)	
Love Life	1.) 2.)	
Family	1.) 2.)	
Spirituality	1.) 2.)	
Friends	1.) 2.)	
Self	1.) 2.)	

Your biggest struggle in all areas combined?

_____

_____

_____

_____

_____

VISUAL WHEEL

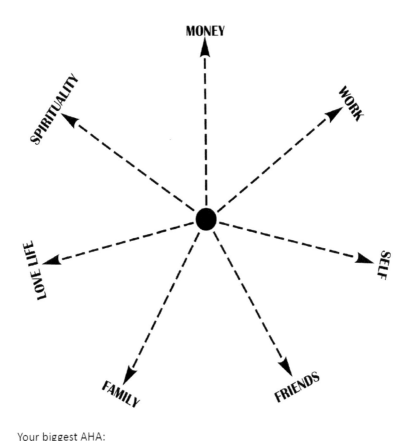

Your biggest AHA:

_____

_____

_____

_____

_____

Where will you be?

7 Boxes of Life

Work
| 1.) |
| 2.) |

Money
| 1.) |
| 2.) |

Love Life
| 1.) |
| 2.) |

Family
| 1.) |
| 2.) |

Spirituality
| 1.) |
| 2.) |

Friends
| 1.) |
| 2.) |

Self
| 1.) |
| 2.) |

Your most important goal to focus on:

_____

_____

_____

_____

_____

CORE Charity

From the inception of The CORE Training, we made charity a part of our culture. At every event we donate to a worthy cause. This comes from the fines our coaches charge when our Level 3 coaching members do not complete their homework assignments. At the end of the semester, The CORE matches the amount, and we give that to a local charity.

We give of our money

Every coaching member also tracks their individual giving amount each month. I am so proud to say that as a company, we donate about $30,000 at each Summit, and in 2015 alone our partners, coaches, and Level 3 coaching members donated $4 million to local charities.

We give of our time

We are committed to not only give of our money, but our time. In September 2015, we introduced our Change the Planet Week initiative. We chose one week where CORE staff and coaching members across the nation took time to volunteer in their local communities.

Constantly striving for greatness

In The CORE, we challenge each other to continual change by walking through our fears to become better people. In challenging our own fears, we strengthen and empower CORE members to face theirs and remember why we all must show up big every day. We are responsible to help those who cannot help themselves, as well as our families and others, in order to be the best versions of ourselves every day!

On the following pages, you will hear from Rick's mentor, Roy Mason. Roy is a minister who runs Global Evangelism Ministries, and has played an integral part in Rick's spiritual development. In turn, Rick has led many of us to live by a higher power, and we are grateful to have Roy lead us in The CORE in our spiritual growth and personal development. We have asked Roy to share with you the key principles we live by at The CORE: gratitude, generosity, and graciousness.

Chaplain Roy Mason:
The Three G's of Living

It is no coincidence that you are reading this book! While you are reading all about tactics and strategies for growing your real estate business, it is vital that you stop and remember three key words that are really the litmus test of life.

All of life can be summed up in three simple words. I call these The 3 G's of Living. There is nothing magical about these words. There is nothing mystical about these words. There is nothing mechanical about these words. These are three words that will serve well to balance and blend your life into true meaningfulness. I challenge you to really consider the words: gratitude, graciousness, and generosity.

Gratitude
"How much is enough?"

You've probably read or heard about this question being asked of John D. Rockefeller. This multi-billionaire replied, "Just a little more!" This whimsical retort sadly reveals the hearts and attitudes of too many people. Material success, however we might measure it, has an illusiveness that can be intoxicating to those who are looking for a definitive way of measuring their lives.

In the hectic thing that is called life, we can easily go through days without thoughts of the blessings of God. Often, though completely without intent, we live our days with an absolute ignorance for all that God is doing around us. We do not awaken each morning with an eye toward heaven. We do not think about the air that we are breathing or the ground on which we are walking, that these are all blessings and provisions from God. Now, intellectually, we know these things are certainly not of our doing, but rarely do we stop and voice a word of thanksgiving for these things. The less we think about God in the small things, the easier it is for us to forget God in the large things.

As we begin to simply take for granted all the natural things in life, the more apt we are to forget God all together. Someone has said that far too many of us traverse through life as practical atheists! This is a sobering and maybe even offensive way of stating it, but I think this is a pretty accurate description. When we go through our day without any acknowledgement of the presence of God in our lives, we are, in fact, a practical atheist for that day. While few would say, "Yes, you're right. I'm an atheist," your lack of constant acknowledgement of His presence proves your testimony.

Many of us need to learn that we are not the owners, but *stewards* of the things of life. When a person believes that he or she alone is the reason for his success or status in life, they are certainly on a slippery slope toward delusion.

Here's what I mean. Suppose a man has been very successful in his business and has accumulated a great deal of wealth. He looks around and sees some of his colleagues and acquaintances who are struggling and having a difficult time. Perhaps these friends turn to him for help. The successful man pauses and contemplates what he should do. If he is not careful, he will simply think about his own hard work and surmise that if the friend worked as hard and was as smart, he would not find himself in his current situation. Thus, the successful man decides to turn a deaf ear to the request. The successful man surmises, "I've worked hard and earned all I have and have made a nice little pile for myself."

Perhaps the successful man is correct in some of his assumptions about the friend, but perhaps God is giving him the opportunity to invest in the man's life the wonderful truths of God. You see, the problem with this line of thinking is that we think are the *owner* of all our possessions. A salient truth of scripture is that God is the owner of everything.

"The earth is the LORD's, and everything in it, the world, and all who live in it;"
— Psalm 24:1 NIV

Is your life marked by the "G" of Gratitude?

Generosity

If we ever grasp the reality that you and I are simply managers for all that God entrusts to us, we will develop a more mature understanding of compassion, concern, and commitment.

Do not read into these last few lines that I am saying we should be foolish and empty-headed about every request that is made of us. We should not. We must carefully and prayerfully consider every request and trust God to direct us as to when and how we are to respond. Not every request that comes to us is from God, but every request should drive us to God.

I have a friend who is very generous with his resources. I have told him over and over that not every need with which he is presented should be accepted. He should rather, receive the request and seek the mind and Word of God in the matter. This has helped him greatly and has actually increased his participation in missions and financial giving. The greatest lesson he has learned is that God is the owner and he is the manager.

I have shared all of this with you as a reminder that we will never really be grateful for what we manage while we turn an indifferent eye toward the things around us. George Bernard Shaw said, "The worst sin towards our fellow creatures is not to hate them, but to be indifferent to them." Are you indifferent to the needs and circumstances around you?

Let me share the example of James. He does not have an abundance of material wealth. He lived the simple life of a rural pastor — always in small churches. His largest annual income did not exceed $20,000 but he is the most generous man I know. This brother never complained. He has traveled with me on overseas ministry projects since 2003. I have lost count of the number of these trips he has made, but he has become a regular and extremely valuable part of our work in West Africa. James is the picture of generosity.

When he unpacks his suitcase in Ghana, I never cease to be amazed at all that is in there. There are more kinds of food, more kinds of candy, more kinds of bibles, more kinds of shirts, and more kinds of baseball hats than seems possible. Very little, if any, of these items are for James. He brings most of these things to distribute to our pastors and friends living in Ghana. Nearly all of the pastors with whom we work wear something that

James has brought to them. These men are walking testimonies to the generosity of this man who has discovered that *"it is more blessed to give than to receive."* (Acts 20:35 NIV)

James has a heart that is engulfed with love. Love for God and love for others is a hallmark of his life. I think it is imperative for us to know that as we love, we give. Too often, many of our lives are not marked by generosity, and this is because we do not really understand love.

Consider this statement: We show who we love by what we do with what we have.

In the midst of his letter to the Christians at Corinth, the Apostle Paul writes, *"If I speak in the tongues of men and of angels, but have not love, I am only a resounding gong or a clanging cymbal. If I have the gift of prophecy and can fathom all mysteries and all knowledge, and if I have a faith that can move mountains, but have not love, I am nothing. If I give all I possess to the poor and surrender my body to the flames, but have not love, I gain nothing.*

Love is patient, love is kind. It does not envy, it does not boast, it is not proud. It is not rude, it is not self-seeking, it is not easily angered, it keeps no record of wrongs. Love does not delight in evil but rejoices with the truth. It always protects, always trusts, always hopes, always perseveres." (1 Cor. 3: 1-7 *NIV*)

Many people have an "I" problem where we are far too concerned with our own satisfaction. Many are afraid that someone might take advantage of us and thus are completely guarded. Out of a distorted view of life, we think that much of our modern world (especially the Western world) operates from a position of self-fulfillment. Look at a simple list of things Paul includes in his paragraph. Here are some simple truths I hope you will consider:

> "Love is patient ... Love is kind ... Love does not boast ... Love is not proud ... Love is not rude ... Love is not self-seeking ... Love is not easily angered ... Love does not keep a record of wrongs..."

Once we know and have this kind of love controlling our hearts, we will become generous in our approach to life. We will be generous with our time, our talents, and our treasures. The millionaires in eternity are the givers in time.

Is your life marked by the "G" of Generosity?

Graciousness

GRACIOUS is a word that is rarely used these days. I am convinced that graciousness is a quality that needs to be more evident in our lives each day.

Graciousness is displayed in kindness and courteousness. It is often easy for us to lack this character trait and excuse it in light of our circumstances, but what must we do?

Graciousness is a matter of the heart and of the mind.

I had someone say to me once that "whatever is in the well will come up in the bucket."

Graciousness is a daily determination to make positive and impactful contributions to others. It is looking for ways to encourage and elevate others even when we are correcting them. It is also knowing how to receive correction in our own lives.

Graciousness is also a matter of the heart! I remember a time in my own life when this point was nailed down while I was traveling overseas on a ministry project. After a particularly difficult overnight flight that had been filled with delays and turmoil, I walked into the Lufthansa lounge in the Munich Airport. As I entered the room and walked to the hospitality desk, I presented my frequent flyer card and boarding pass to the lady at the desk. When I say "presented," I really mean I threw the two items onto her desk. My complete lack of graciousness was met by her remark, "You don't have to throw it at me!" This only served to fuel my own fleshly reaction of "I did not throw it at you!" She now entered into a bit of banter with me, which only took me further down the wrong path. I finally said, "You know, there are lots of lounges in this airport" and I huffed off.

My ministry colleague and friend immediately chastised me and said, "Roy, you are being horrible to that person!" After sitting down for a moment in the lounge, I realized I had, in fact, been horrible and walked back to the desk to apologize to the hostess. Much to my chagrin, when I got back to the desk, she was nowhere to be found. Embarrassed, ashamed, and internally broken, I asked for the woman, and her replacement informed me her shift had ended and she had gone home. *"Great,"* I thought. *"Now my chance to make this right is gone."*

I had allowed the temporary circumstances of life to lead me down a bad path. I was not made to act this way toward the woman in the lounge. I had chosen to act this way. It was not my fault, but it was my problem. I felt all of what Romans 8:15 says, "I do not understand what I do. For what I want to do, I do not do, but what I hate, I do."

We all have the potential to do the wrong thing. I had chosen poorly.

I made up my mind on that day that I would do all within my power to never let this kind of thing happen again. I prayed and asked God to keep me from falling and giving into the temptation of taking things into my own hands. I cannot say that I have never failed again, but I can tell you that God used that moment in my life to make me mindful and aware of both my nature and His nature.

Two years later, I was walking into that same Lufthansa lounge in Munich with my same ministry colleague. As the doors slide open he said to me, "Roy! There's she is." He was right. It was the same woman with whom I had lost my witness twenty-four months earlier. I had a choice to make. Would I bring it up to this woman whom I was sure would not remember me, or would I simply be nice this time? It was clear in my spirit that I needed ask this woman to forgive me.

As I approached the desk I smiled and said, "Ma'am, I want to apologize to you."

She looked at me with confused eyes and asked, "For what?"

I said, "Two years ago in this very lounge I was rude and ugly to you. That was not the way you should have been treated, and it is not the way I should have acted, and I hope you will forgive me."

With a slack jaw and teary eyes she said, "I do not remember ... but thank you!"

"I am Christian, and on that day I did not display the nature of Christ," I continued. "And I am truly sorry for my attitude."

Now nearly weeping, she said, "No one has ever apologized for the things they've said to me! Certainly, I forgive you."

While it would be preferable to never have to eat our own words, there will come a time when all of us have to do so. Maybe there is someone right now with whom you have not been gracious. As God gives you the opportunity, display the truth of graciousness to them.

Now here's the question. When faced with challenges and obstacles, do you react or respond? Remember, reactions, while natural, are selfish and circumstantial. When we react, we are simply doing what anybody does. Are you simply a person of circumstances? Are you simply a selfish person?

Responses are spiritual choices. So being gracious is not only a matter of the heart, but it is a matter of the head.

We can choose to default to the flesh or surrender to the spirit. We react from our flesh, but we respond from our spirit. You have a choice EVERY TIME to allow the spirit of Christ to respond through you. I hope today you will join me in asking God to develop a gracious spirit within us so that God might be gloried in all that we do.

Is your life marked by the "G" of Graciousness?

As your life is working toward fulfillment, I hope you will consider these three words and ask God to make you a "3 G" person.

SECTION FIVE:
CLOSING
THOUGHTS

RICK RUBY'S CLOSING THOUGHTS

I think real estate sales is a great career. I think most agents treat real estate like a hobby. They don't run it like a career. If you come with The CORE, I'm going to teach you how to build a business, prospect automatically, how to build a team to support you, and how to prepare a Profit & Loss statement and a personal budget. You will have money in the bank, and you will have a future to retire on. Over time, about two to three years later, I will teach you how to have full life balance, have fun, recreate, and have it all, but in the beginning, you are going to have to work really hard to set these systems up to build a business.

Earlier I mentioned the book *The E-Myth* by Michael Gerber. It's about how to go from technician to business person. Right now, most of you reading this book as real estate agents are technicians. You are fun, charming, and out there, flying by the seat of your pants. You are doing some deals and having some fun. You are making some money, but you're exhausted.

I'm talking about being a dialed-in business person where other people do half of the work and, eventually, other people will do all of the work. Now, where I am in my life, other people do 70% of my work. I do about 30% of my own work. In the next five years, I'm going to get it to the point where other people do 90% of my work and I do 10%. If I don't get to that, I will burn out and retire.

Real estate is a great career. You can have it all and make a lot of money. You can be in love and be physically fit, but the journey is going to be like climbing Mount Everest, and only a few are committed to going all of the way.

Thank you for reading this book. I hope you enjoyed it. You are in the right career, but we need to make a lot of changes to the path. Many in your industry are confused. I believe The CORE has the answers to help you live out your fullest potential. Come check us out!

RECOMMENDED BOOKS

At The CORE, we strive for constant improvement in both our personal and business lives. Below you will find a list of books recommended by our coaches. The ones in bold are Rick Ruby's personal favorites that he considers essential for any business person striving for breakout success.

- ***Raving Fans: A Revolutionary Approach to Customer Service*** by Ken Blanchard and Sheldon Bowles
- ***E-myth: Why Most Small Businesses Don't Work and What to Do About It*** by Michael Gerber
- ***Who Moved My Cheese: An Amazing Way to Deal With Change in Your Work and in Your Life*** *by Spencer Johnson and Kenneth Blanchard*
- ***The Five Love Languages: The Secret to Love that Lasts*** by Gary Chapman
- ***The Greatest Salesman in the World*** by Og Mandino
- ***Lead, for God's Sake! A Parable for Finding the Heart of Leadership*** by Todd Gongwer
- ***Mr. Shmooze: The Art and Science of Selling Through Relationships*** by Richard Abraham
- *5 Languages of Appreciation in the Workplace: Empowering Organizations by Encouraging People* by Gary Chapman and Paul White
- *5 Levels of Leadership: Proven Steps to Maximize Your Potential* by John C. Maxwell
- *21 Indispensable Qualities of a Leader: Becoming the Person Others Will Want to Follow* by John Maxwell
- *Being in Balance: 9 Principles for Creating Habits to Match Your Desires* by Dr. Wayne Dyer

- *Energy Bus: 10 Rules to Fuel Your Life, Work, and Team with Positive Energy* by Jon Gordon
- *Go for No! Yes is the Destination, No is How You Get There* by Andrea Waltz and Richard Fenton
- *The Go-Giver: A Little Story About a Powerful Business Idea* by Bob Burg and John David Mann
- *Great Leaders Grow: Becoming a Leader for Life* by Ken Blanchard and Mark Miller
- *The One-Minute Manager* by Keith Blanchard and Spencer Johnson
- *Small Giants: Companies that Choose to be Great Instead of Big* by Bo Burlingham
- *Strengths Finder* by Tom Rath
- *Take the Stairs: 7 Steps to Achieving True Success* by Rory Vaden
- *Topgrading: How to Hire, Coach, and Keep A Players* by Brad Smart and Geoff Smart

RECOMMENDED MOVIES AND TELEVISION

There is a lot we can learn from the stories told in movies and television shows. For Rick Ruby, *Pay It Forward* is a foundational movie for how each coaching member should live their life.

Movies
- ***Pay It Forward*** (2000)
- *Coach Carter* (2005)
- *Miracle* (2004)
- *Door to Door* (TV movie, 2002)

Television
- *The Profit* (on CNBC)
- *Million Dollar Listing* (on Bravo)

REETA CASEY: WHY HAVE A COACH?

You got into this business because you like being independent. You don't want someone telling you what to do. We understand. All our real estate coaches and coaching students, myself included, has been there.

Accountability takes you to the top
Take a look at the Real Estate Agent Development Process below. If you have the right amount of determination and drive, you can go far on your own. But only so far. The key ingredient in coaching with The CORE is accountability. Being held accountable to your coach, to your fellow coaching members, and to your own goals will push you to the next level, the one you've only thought possible in your dreams.

Breaking out of the box and truly changing your mindset about how to think and run your business takes strong leadership. At The CORE, we have the programs, the structure, and the community to initiate and sustain that change. If you love real estate but are frustrated with the hours you are working, your personal money, or your personal production, call us NOW.

Our coaching programs
We are an elite coaching company unlike any other. Our coaches are active in the business and coach from the "biggest pile" theory, meaning that each student is coached by someone who has more production or cash.

We have programs for wherever you are at in your business, from the 12 Step Program, the Next 24 Program, Level 1.5 coaching, the Summit, and finally, our elite two-year Level 3 coaching.

What success looks like

The CORE Training has produced some incredible real estate agents who not only net $500,000 to $1.2 million, but they do it in 35 to 45 hours a week and enjoy their life and family. If you are committed to being the best you can be, to helping people pay it forward, and are coachable, then you are exactly who The CORE Training is looking for. Join us and become part of our culture, which is changing the real estate industry through amazing, committed agents.

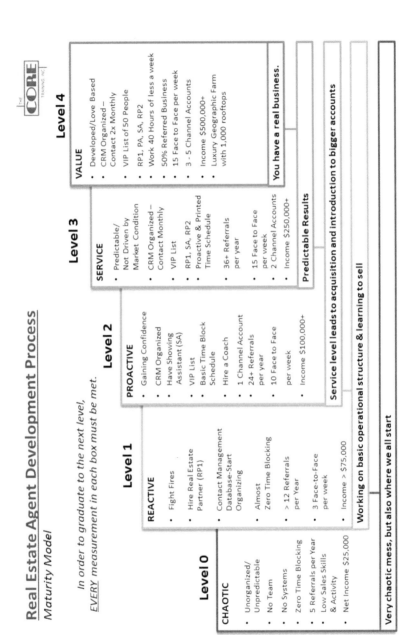

Real Estate Agent Development Process
Maturity Model

In order to graduate to the next level,
EVERY measurement in each box must be met.

Level 0
CHAOTIC
- Unorganized/Unpredictable
- No Team
- No Systems
- Zero Time Blocking
- 5 Referrals per Year
- Low Sales Skills & Activity
- Net Income $25,000

Very chaotic mess, but also where we all start

Level 1
REACTIVE
- Fight Fires
- Hire Real Estate Partner (RP1)
- Contact Management Database-Start Organizing
- Almost Zero Time Blocking
- > 12 Referrals per Year
- 3 Face-to-Face per week
- Income > $75,000

Working on basic operational structure & learning to sell

Level 2
PROACTIVE
- Gaining Confidence
- CRM Organized
- Have Showing Assistant (SA)
- VIP List
- Basic Time Block Schedule
- Hire a Coach
- 1 Channel Account
- 24+ Referrals per year
- 10 Face to Face per week
- Income $100,000+

Service level leads to acquisition and introduction to bigger accounts

Level 3
SERVICE
- Predictable/Not Driven by Market Condition
- CRM Organized – Contact Monthly
- VIP List
- RP1, SA, RP2
- Proactive & Printed Time Schedule
- 36+ Referrals per year
- 15 Face to Face per week
- 2 Channel Accounts
- Income $250,000+

Predictable Results

Level 4
VALUE
- Developed/Love Based
- CRM Organized – Contact 2x Monthly
- VIP List of 50 People
- RP1, PA, SA, RP2
- Work 40 Hours of less a week
- 50% Referred Business
- 15 Face to Face per week
- 3 - 5 Channel Accounts
- Income $500,000+
- Luxury Geographic Farm with 1,000 rooftops

You have a real business.

HOW TO CONTACT THE CORE TRAINING

For more information, visit our website at www.thecoretraining.com, or call 1-800-660-6670.

If you want to know how we help agents like you, then order *Our CORE Journey* and read the stories of other real estate agents. How exciting to know there is a coaching company that is different, A company that lives by what it teaches, limits its relationships to ensure a great client experience, whose coaches are active in the business and have achieved more in production, cash net worth, or savings.

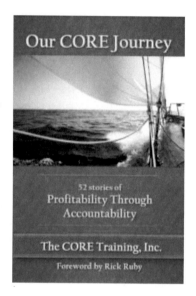

Our CORE Journey

52 stories of
Profitability Through
Accountability

The CORE Training, Inc.

Foreword by Rick Ruby

Last Thoughts from Reeta Casey

For me, the journey has been amazing. I am living my dream with my husband and looking forward to years of working with The CORE and my charities. If you want to create your dream life, we can show you the way. We have a proven path and the success stories to support it. Change requires a new culture, systems and structure, and accountability. We can help if you are ready to put forth the effort. Connect today because you should be on the path to create the business and life you want!

OUR PROGRAMS AND PRODUCTS

12 Steps to Double Your Income

1. 12-step tracking and business boosting system (online and workbook)
2. Greatness Tracker
3. Access to member site and online library
4. Mobile app

The Next 24

1. 12 steps for that continues with the basics with a focus on building your team (online and workbook)
2. Action video for each step
3. Greatness Tracker
4. Access to member site and online library
5. Mobile app

The Blue Beast Workbook

Organize and track your business results with the Blue Beast Workbook. Included in the workbook are:

1. Things To Do Today
2. Pay Log
3. Phone Log
4. Profit & Loss
5. Lead Tracker
6. Personal Budget

Each Blue Beast also includes a guide and the *Six Steps to Financial Freedom* CD.

The Summit

Our revolutionary events are systematically designed to change and improve your business immediately. This two-day event will immerse you in all of The CORE Training's tactics, systems, and structures.

Level 3 Coaching

Our two-year program tracks your business results through our proven systems and an intense dose of accountability. In this program, three coaching members participate in a bi-monthly call with a top-producing coach. You must qualify for and attend a Summit to apply for Level 3 coaching.

www.thecoretraining.com